Avro 748

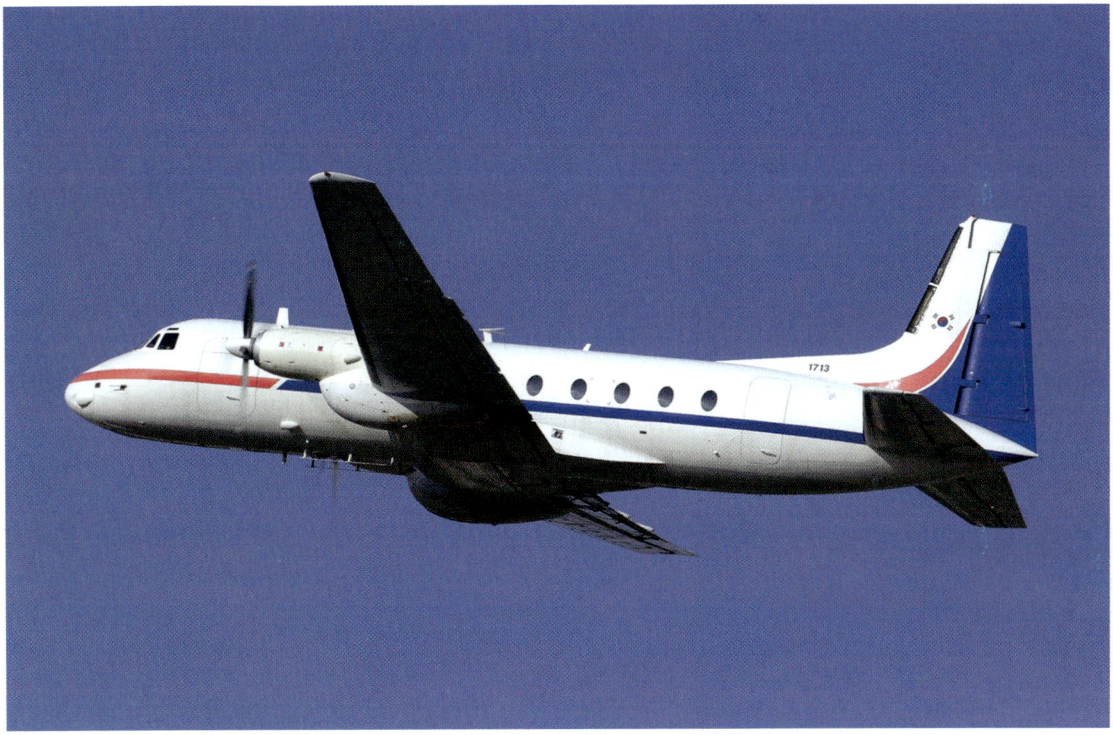

BARRY LLOYD

HISTORIC COMMERCIAL AIRCRAFT SERIES, VOLUME 3

Title page image: The colour scheme almost suggests a commercial airliner but, in fact, serial 1713, a Series 2A, was operated by the Korean Air Force. (4 Aviation)

Contents page image: Unloading cargo, Guyana style, at the airfield in Lethem. The 748s were used as combination aircraft, and there was never any shortage of cargo. (Author)

Published by Key Books
An imprint of Key Publishing Ltd
PO Box 100
Stamford
Lincs PE19 1XQ

www.keypublishing.com

The right of Barry Lloyd to be identified as the author of this book has been asserted in accordance with the Copyright, Designs and Patents Act 1988 Sections 77 and 78.

Copyright © Barry Lloyd, 2021

ISBN 978 1 913870 87 4

All rights reserved. Reproduction in whole or in part in any form whatsoever or by any means is strictly prohibited without the prior permission of the Publisher.

Typeset by SJmagic DESIGN SERVICES, India.

Contents

Introduction 4

Chapter 1   Europe 16

Chapter 2   Africa 30

Chapter 3   Middle East and Asia 42

Chapter 4   Australasia and Oceania 53

Chapter 5   North America 61

Chapter 6   Latin America and the Caribbean 75

Introduction

The intention of this publication is to take the reader from the origins of the 748, through some of the worldwide, and largely successful, selling campaigns to both civil and military operators and detail some of the lesser-known background stories to one of the most successful British airliners.

As the jet age approached in the 1960s, operators who had fleets of piston-engined, unpressurised aircraft began to look for more modern versions of the aircraft that had served them so well in the post-war years. Aircraft manufacturers were quickly tuned in to the needs of the operators and began to see the potential for designing and building new civil aircraft, which would incorporate the latest developments in aviation technology. The aircraft that was top of the replacement list was the DC-3, and A V Roe, commonly known as Avro, based in Manchester, set about designing an aircraft to take its place.

With fuel-efficient and reliable turboprop engines now available, and with the ability to fully pressurise the cabin, operators were quick to realise the benefits that such innovations could bring, both for themselves and their passengers. Avro was not alone in this endeavour, however, since several other British and foreign aircraft manufacturers were also quick to realise the possibilities.

The 748 actually needs little introduction. It has carried the registrations of more than 100 countries and the colours of more than 80 operators. From the beginning, the aircraft offered versatility. Apart from its principal role as an airliner, it has been adapted to become a VIP transport, specifically for heads of state, and it was converted for maritime surveillance, as a freighter, a paratrooper, an electronics platform, a calibration aircraft, an airborne surveillance platform and, more recently, a water-bomber. Some were even privately owned. It is a tribute to its rugged construction that, more than 30 years after the last new aircraft was delivered, there are a number of examples still in operation, chiefly in Canada and parts of Africa.

The aircraft that the 748 was designed to replace, although few were kept in as immaculate condition as this example in Costa Rica. (Author)

Introduction

Knowing that it would sell in countries where support facilities were limited, it was designed for easy maintenance. Access to the engines and undercarriage was straightforward and, wherever possible, simplicity was incorporated into the design. Later models had engines equipped with water methanol injection – a system designed to increase take-off power, particularly from airfields that are situated at altitude in countries with warm climates. The 748 underwent a policy of continuous improvement, with increased engine power and aerodynamic improvements, culminating in the Series 2B. From the original design came the development of the Andover, a larger version of the aircraft adapted specifically for military use, of which more than 30 were built. The military was an obvious target for the 748, and in the early 1960s, an invitation to tender for 31 military freighters had been issued. Avro had claimed that the 748 could operate from virtually any surface, so the Royal Air Force arranged a trial against the Handley Page Herald. The chosen venue was the airfield at RAF Martlesham Heath in Suffolk, but the standard runway would not be used. Prior to the day of the trial, a strip 30 yards (27m) wide had been ploughed parallel to the main runway, and there had been rain overnight, so the landing area was wet and rutted. Undeterred, the contenders took their turns, but the 748 won by a significant margin. From this, the Andover was eventually developed, featuring the rear-loading door requested by the Ministry of Defence.

There was no shortage of competitors for the 748. Fokker, of the Netherlands, introduced the F-27, also built under licence in the USA as the Fairchild Hiller FH-227, an independently developed version, with a 6ft (1.83m) stretch, enabling seating capacity to be increased to 56. Additionally, de Havilland Canada produced 113 examples of the DHC-7, known more familiarly as the Dash 7. This was followed by its twin-engined cousin, known as the Dash 8, which first appeared in 1983 and is still in production, having, like the 748, gone through several changes of manufacturing ownership since it was first introduced. The Japanese introduced the YS-11, which, although having a greater seating capacity than the 748, was often considered as a competitor by both manufacturer and customer. Most of them saw service with Japanese operators, although several operators – Aerolíneas Argentinas, Bouraq of Indonesia, and Philippine Airlines – operated both the 748 and the YS-11. Production was terminated after 180 were built. The Convair 580, a turboprop conversion of the earlier Convair series,

G-ARRV was originally built as a Series 1 and registered G-APZV. It was later adapted as the HS 780 Andover prototype. (David R Lawrence)

Although larger than the 748, the YS-11 was seen as a competitor. Most of the sales were in Southeast Asia, with 180 being built. (Bob O'Brien Collection)

The STOL capabilities of the Dash 7 were a useful selling point, and it was used to great effect in the early days of London City Airport. (Author)

saw widespread service in North America, prior to the 748 receiving Federal Aviation Administration (FAA) certification. In more recent years, the turboprop of choice has become the Avions de Transport Régional (ATR) 42 with 42-plus seats and, later, the 70-seater ATR 72, which is now seen in all corners of the world.

History

News reached Avro that Fokker was also planning to introduce a similar-sized aircraft, also with the Rolls-Royce Dart engine, which would make it a direct competitor with the 748. Fokker had chosen a high-wing design, thus requiring strengthening of the fuselage, resulting in an increase in weight. Also, the high wing would mean that the fuselage was closer to the ground and, thus, not as suitable for operation into unpaved airfields.

Initial production of the 748 took place at the factory in Chadderton, in north Manchester, but this facility did not have an airfield, so once completed, the wings and fuselage sections were taken the 18 miles (29km) by road to the final assembly unit at Woodford. This had to be done at a time when

Above: The F-27 outsold the 748. However, its high wing and low-slung fuselage meant that it was unsuitable for unprepared runways. (Bob O'Brien Collection)

Right: The wings and fuselages of the 748 were built at Chadderton and conveyed to Woodford by road. (Keir J Faulkner)

there were low volumes of traffic, because the trailer required to move the airframe was 40ft (12m) long, and corners and roundabouts had to be carefully negotiated, often the wrong way round, and sometimes with a police escort.

With one eye on the rugged field capability of the DC-3, the designers at Avro set about looking at how a modern aircraft could also achieve the same operational capabilities whilst improving its ability to operate from unpaved strips. A full galley would be provided, together with a typical seating capacity of 48 – almost twice that of the DC-3. Existing DC-3 operators were canvassed for their opinions and a general outline began to take shape.

Development

In January 1959, the Avro board took a decision to back the project. It was proposed as a private venture with no government funding. The Rolls-Royce Dart engine, already successful on the Vickers Viscount and Fokker F-27, was chosen as the powerplant. Detailed design work began shortly afterwards, and on 24 June 1960, the first prototype, G-APZV, took to the air. All was going well until there were a series of fires at the Chadderton factory during 1959 and 1960. In the last of these,

The original demonstrator aircraft, G-ARAY wore at least ten colour schemes during its life. The last one was that of Dan-Air. (Bob O'Brien Collection)

considerable damage was done to the fuselages destined to become the prototype and test airframes, thus delaying the programme by about six months.

Although delayed, flight testing and certification continued, and the flight trials were completed by November 1961. The Series 1 748 was finally issued with a Certificate of Airworthiness in July 1962. Various improvements had been made to the production aircraft, with increases to the wingspan and an uprated Dart engine. The 748 underwent a continuous development programme and on 6 November 1961, G-ARAY, the second prototype aircraft, made its first flight as a Series 2 aircraft. This was then used for a number of years as the demonstrator aircraft, including being leased out to several potential operators. The name 'Avro Ltd' ceased to exist on 1 July 1963, when it became part of Hawker Siddeley Aviation Ltd, together with Armstrong Whitworth, de Havilland and Hawker. Hawker Siddeley itself became part of British Aerospace in 1977 when the industry was nationalised.

Sales

Once the initial orders had been received, there was something of a lull for a year or two until 1964, when orders from both UK and foreign operators began to materialise. A second aircraft, G-ATAM, built as a Series 2 aircraft, was also used as a demonstrator and leased out to potential operators. The go-anywhere capability of the 748 had not gone unnoticed by senior figures in government, and it was not long before requests began to be made for VIP interior fits for heads of state. Among the early customers were The Queen's Flight of the Royal Air Force. The Royal Australian Air Force (RAAF), were also early customers, followed by the Royal Thai Air Force. In South America, the presidents of Venezuela and Argentina placed orders, as did the Zambia Air Force in Africa. The one thing these countries had in common was their warm and humid climates, and the air conditioning, which had been designed initially to deal with a northern European climate, was insufficient. A solution was achieved by fitting an auxiliary power unit (APU) to the starboard engine. This was housed in a fairing above the engine cowling. The APU was built by Rover, a British car manufacturer at that time, and was able to provide start-up power to the engines and operate the air conditioning system whilst the aircraft was on the ground. The weight penalty for having this item installed was minimal, and since the aircraft were in VIP configuration, they would not be subject to the same weight limits as a typical airliner.

The continual development process brought about further modifications to the design, and in 1967, a Series 2A was launched. This aircraft had the benefit of a more powerful version of the Dart engine, thereby offering higher landing and take-off weights, thus enabling higher payloads. Many of the aircraft originally supplied as Series 2s underwent the modification, and by 1969, all the standard production aircraft were built as Series 2As. The success of the 748 resulted in Hawker Siddeley winning the Queen's Award for

An immaculate Series 2 example, PI-C1021 sits in the hangar at Woodford prior to delivery in 1968. (Gerry Manning)

Industry in 1970. This was in recognition of the export sales of the aircraft, which now counted operators in countries as diverse as Australia, Brazil, Malawi, Mexico, Nepal, and the Philippines amongst its customers. By now, some operators were beginning to replace the 748 with either newer models or a larger, usually jet, type. This meant that the used aircraft were able to find new markets. One airline in particular, Dan-Air of the UK, became one of the early customers for such aircraft. Dan-Air had a very capable engineering division that was ideally suited to converting the 748 for its operations.

US Certification

The US was one market that had not been penetrated at this point. It had been complicated by the fact that Fokker had concluded an agreement with the US manufacturer Fairchild to build and market the F-27 under licence, thus giving it easy access into the market. Additionally, Fairchild, in co-operation with Hiller, built a stretched version of the F-27, known as the FH-227. The FH-227 was a larger aircraft, having a 6ft (1.83m) stretch over the F-27, and offering 56 seats in the standard version. The Japanese YS-11, similar in design to the 748 but offering a larger fuselage and seating for 64 passengers, had also made some inroads into the US market, with airlines such as Piedmont and Provincetown-Boston Airlines. An additional obstacle to sales in the US was the need for FAA certification. In order for the 748 to obtain FAA approval, it was necessary for a number of modifications to be made. The process was costly, but ultimately proved to be worthwhile. The first aircraft was delivered to Air Illinois at its base in Carbondale in January 1973. However, there was an added complication. Air Illinois wanted to operate the aircraft out of Meigs Field, a conveniently located downtown airport in Chicago, normally used for general aviation. The FAA, doubtful of the 748's ability to use the 3,900 x 150ft (1,189 x 46m) strip on Northerly Island, an artificial peninsula on the edge of Lake Michigan, insisted on a demonstration. A successful demonstration ensured that approval was given, and the 748 became the largest aircraft to operate scheduled services from the airport, but, in fact, the exercise proved academic. Whilst the Air Illinois 748s operated successfully in and out of Meigs Field for a number of years, the mayor of Chicago saw things differently. In 1994, he announced that the airport would be closed, and a park built on the site. After much debate, in 2001, a compromise was reached between the parties concerned for the airport to remain open for another 25 years. However, the US Senate did not approve the agreement, and on 30 March 2003, Mayor Daley ordered the drilling of large X-shaped gouges into the runway surface in the middle of the night. A demolition notice, required by law, was not given to the FAA; as a result, 16 light aircraft were left stranded at the airport and inbound flights had to be diverted by air traffic control

Displaying its show number, G-BKLD is seen here in Bouraq colours at Le Bourget in May 1983. (Gerry Manning)

because of equipment scattered on the runway. The 16 stranded aircraft were later allowed to depart using Meigs' 3,000ft (914m) parallel taxiway, but scheduled airline services had to be terminated.

Large Freight Doors

As the design teams worked on improvements for the Series 2 aircraft, it was becoming apparent from enquires, particularly from existing military operators, that there was a requirement for a large freight door (LFD). This could be used for dropping parachutists and supplies. With this in mind, plans were drawn up and submitted for approval. One of the early requests had come from the Brazilian Air Force (FAB), whose aircraft were well down the production stage, but still at a point where the conversion could take place. Prior to this, a considerable number of trials were necessary, and an LFD was fitted to another production aircraft, G-AZJH. This was done during 1971, with trials taking place during 1972, including taking the aircraft to India, where supply dropping and parachute trials were handled successfully. Certification was obtained and six Series 2A production aircraft, the second batch to be delivered to the FAB, were all fitted with LFDs and delivered during 1975. The door was designed in

CS-03 of the Belgian Air Force, operated by 21 Sqn based at Melsbroek, seen here at Farnborough in September 1976. (Gerry Manning)

such a way that the rear passenger door could be operated independently when the aircraft was in an all-passenger configuration. When the cargo door needed to be opened, it would slide forward, thus providing a working area that was 8ft 9in (2.67m) wide and 5ft 8in (1.75m) high. The LFD was an option taken up by most of the military operators of the 748, but a number of civil operators in less developed nations also took advantage of the modification. At a time when road transport was difficult and dangerous, large and valuable cargo could easily be carried in the cabin of the aircraft, with the forward area being used for passenger seating, or, if there was a large volume of freight, the seats could easily be removed, and the aircraft could quickly become a complete freighter capable of uplifting up to six tonnes.

Coastguarder

With their history of developing maritime patrol aircraft, such as the Shackleton and the Nimrod, it was perhaps inevitable that the Manchester factories would consider the 748 as an alternative aircraft for this purpose. During the 1970s, exclusive economic zones (EEZs) were set up around the world, in order to protect the fishing and mineral rights of maritime nations. The EEZs were set at 200 nautical miles, thus making surface patrols time-consuming and expensive. With its low-wing configuration, the 748 was considered a stable platform for low-level operations over the sea, and its large cabin would easily enable the fitting of whatever equipment was required for the task.

A Series 2A had been sold to Copa Airlines in Panama in May 1969, but it had never fully fitted into its operating programme and was later stored in Bolivia following a frustrated sale. It was bought back by Hawker Siddeley and returned to Woodford in May 1975, with a view to convert it into a Coastguarder demonstrator. Registered G-BCDZ, it was used as a trials and demonstrator aircraft. In the meantime, design drawings had been produced and the aircraft was flown to another Hawker Siddeley factory at Hawarden, near Chester, in February 1976, for conversion. The aircraft retained the standard passenger door, with the most visible differences externally being a 'chin' radome under the forward loading door, and blister windows replacing the standard fitting on either side of the penultimate windows. These enabled a much clearer view below the aircraft. There followed numerous demonstration tours, including an appearance at Farnborough Air Show in 1978 and the Paris Air Show the following year. However, the response was lukewarm, with many countries opting to keep whatever equipment they had or buying a smaller aircraft for maritime patrol.

The original Coastguarder, G-BCDZ, seen in the static park at Farnborough in September 1978. (Gerry Manning)

Waiting for customs clearance at Narsarsuaq, Greenland, G-BDVH is on its way to South America for a demo tour. (Author)

On this basis, the idea was discontinued by the end of 1979, and the aircraft returned to its original passenger-carrying condition and was used for trials, demonstrations, and leases. The idea was not entirely forgotten, however, because in 1981, word reached the pilots' office in Woodford that there was to be a competition, called 'Sea Search '81', which would form part of the Greenham Common Air Show. There were to be 31 entrants for the competition, from all over the world, consisting of expert maritime patrol teams, all of them military and all of them using their best available equipment, with aircraft attending from as far away as Argentina. With their tongues firmly in their cheeks, the office staff sent off an application form and, to their surprise, the application was accepted. It was an even greater surprise when the scratch team from Woodford won, even outflanking the Nimrod.

The aircraft chosen was G-BDVH, a standard production 748 Series 2A, which had been fitted with an LFD. It was no stranger to demonstration flights, however, having once been used to demonstrate its ability to land on the tidal beach at Barra in the Outer Hebrides. However, its primary purpose was as a military demonstrator, and it had undertaken a number of foreign tours since coming off the production line in 1976, and later spent periods as a lease aircraft with Air Madagascar and

Seen here in Bouraq colours, but without the titling, and carrying its class B registration, the Series 2B was at Farnborough in September 1982. (Gerry Manning)

Introduction

Bahamasair. In early 1980, it had been converted to what was now being marketed as a 'multi-role' aircraft. This included, amongst other equipment, Searchwater radar, developed by Thorn EMI, a fitting for an Agiflite 70mm precision camera and a sonar-buoy listening-device launch system. It had been painted a drab olive green and was demonstrated at Farnborough in 1980 in full multi-role configuration. Several other demonstration tours followed, but, despite having won the Sea Search competition, there were no sales. The aircraft reverted to civil use and was used as a demonstrator before being sold to the Sri Lankan Air Force in 1986.

As will become evident throughout the book, the 748 became the aircraft of choice for island-based operators around the world. The combination of its rugged airframe and the reliable Rolls-Royce Dart engines played a significant part in the decision-making process of both existing and would-be island operators, such as Indonesia's Bouraq and Merpati, Bahamasair, British Airways Highlands Division, Leeward Islands Air Transport and Philippine Airlines amongst many others.

Series 2B

The philosophy of continuous improvement of the 748 continued throughout its manufacturing life. In June 1979, G-BGJV, the first production version of the Series 2B, took to the skies. The improvements were significant, but not immediately visible. The most important benefits were a reduction in fuel consumption, to combat the rapidly rising fuel prices at the time, together with engine and aerodynamic improvements, and incorporation of the latest technology available on the flight deck. An extended wingspan and a more powerful version of the Dart engine completed the picture. Internally, passenger comfort had not been forgotten. Surprising as it may seem, the internal cabin dimensions of the 748 are similar to those of Concorde. Concorde has an 8ft 6in (2.59m) interior width against 8ft 1in (2.46m) in the 748. Whilst the height in the Concorde cabin is 6ft 5in (1.96m), that of the 748 is 6ft 4in (1.93m). On that basis, it seemed logical to design the new interior based on its supersonic stablemate. Improved cabin insulation and acoustic bulkheads in the forward area dampened the noise and vibration levels in the cabin.

It was time to take the Series 2B on a demonstration tour, with G-BGJV sporting a striking red, white and blue paint scheme, and with FAA type certification confirmed, it was flown to North America in the autumn of 1980 for a major tour. British Aerospace had formed a subsidiary company known as BAe Inc. and, in co-operation with Rolls-Royce, had opened a spares, support and sales facility at Dulles Airport in Washington, DC. The spares holding was built up to serve operators of the aircraft in North America and the Caribbean. Additionally, it was recognised that commuter airlines did not have the deep pockets of the larger national operators, and it was decided that, in order to reduce production

This is the finished article. The 2B demonstrator in its eye-catching colour scheme. (Shaun Connor)

costs, an agreement would be made with a US-based company for the aircraft to be flown there for final completion. Thus, the aircraft completed at Woodford would be flown 'green' – this refers to the coat of oxidised paint that is applied to the aircraft during the production process – to a facility in the US, where specific modifications required for FAA certification and the fitting out of the interiors to the customers' specifications would take place.

Used Aircraft Sales

In some respects, aircraft selling is not that dissimilar from that of any other moveable, high-value asset. Many of the operators choose to exchange or replace them at a given time in their ownership; the reasons for which vary widely. Just as in the case of buying a used car, there is always a deal to be made with the trade-in, especially where an operator wishes to continue with the same type of equipment. A number of operators replaced earlier 748 models with improved versions and, as part of the deal, the earlier models were taken in part-exchange. Among the benefits of this were an existing spares supply, no additional crew training and little or no new maintenance equipment required. The traded-in aircraft then became the property and, therefore, the responsibility of the manufacturer. So, what were they to do with them? Actually, there was never any shortage of interest in used 748s. They had acquired a pedigree; maintenance was simple and, therefore, economical and the aircraft had an excellent reliability record. Start-up airlines were always interested in picking up less expensive aircraft with which to build up their operations. The 748 also became the aircraft of choice for second- and third-level operators around the world. The reputation of the aircraft, reinforced by leases to prospective airlines, played a significant part in the decision-making process of both existing and would-be operators, such as Aeropostal of Venezuela, Bahamasair, British Airways Highlands Division, Varig of Brazil and Aerolíneas Argentinas.

From the manufacturer's point of view, there were always several operators who kept a close eye on the used aircraft market, either to refurbish and sell on to another operator or to augment their own fleets. If the market was sluggish, there was often the possibly of offering it on a short-term lease to an existing operator or maybe to tidy it up for use as a demonstrator or lease aircraft, specifically tailored as part of an ongoing sales campaign. Of the potential used-aircraft buyers, Dan-Air was one of the biggest. All its aircraft were obtained from the used market and no less than 21 748s went through its hands during the airline's existence. Another UK operator, Emerald Airways, who, in fact, bought some of the Dan-Air 748s, had operated a fleet of 23 aircraft when it closed down in 2006.

While detailed histories of the 748 have received excellent coverage, this book aims to shed a rather different light on this popular aircraft by unveiling some of the previously unheard-of background stories behind the sales activities – most successful but a few unsuccessful – of this aircraft, known worldwide as the 'Avro' and sometimes as the 'Budgie', and to offer a wider appreciation of its exceptional working life, especially in some of the more remote parts of the world.

Varig operated 11 748s, which were used initially to open services into the interior of Brazil. All were supplied as Series 2s but later converted to 2As. (David R Lawrence)

Deliveries and Demonstrations

It is self-evident that the 748 was never designed to fly long distances. The maximum range of a Series 2A was 1,700 nautical miles (3,148km). Given that the aircraft would have few people on board, the maximum range would be easily achievable, but if the aircraft was delivered or demonstrated on the other side of the world, the system for achieving this is considerably different.

For the flights to the Americas, there was a fairly standard routing. The first stop would be Reykjavik, in the days when the airport was still open to commercial traffic. The next stop would be Greenland, normally Narsarsuaq, and then on to St John's or Gander in Newfoundland, or perhaps Sept-Îles in the Quebec province, depending on how strong the ever-present headwinds were. If the flight was going further south, the next stop would be Washington DC, where if any spares were required, they were available at the BAe/Rolls-Royce facility there. The refuelling stops were carefully considered for two main factors: weather and alternate airfields. From a fuel point of view, the north Atlantic route was never a problem, but the weather could change quickly and dramatically. Narsarsuaq, tucked into the top of a fjord, is not an easy airfield at the best of times, and any indication of bad weather normally meant a delay from the departure airport until there was a significant improvement. A third factor also had to be added into the equation. Itinerant aircraft are not really welcome at busy major airports and the simple act of handling – customs clearance, refuelling etc – becomes more time-consuming and expensive because of this. For example, if a stop in Florida was required, it would be in either Fort Lauderdale or Opa-Locka rather than Miami or Orlando. Assuming daytime flying only, it would typically take five days to reach the northern countries of South America, such as Colombia.

For eastbound flights, there was a similar tried-and-tested routing. Nice would often be the first stop, followed by Corfu, or maybe Crete, depending on the winds. The next stop would usually be Luxor, in Egypt, and then onto the Gulf before crossing the Arabian Sea and on to the Indian sub-continent. The governing factor here was the weather, as all the transit stops would be chosen for their normally reliable meteorological conditions and the fact that fuel was invariably available. Fuel was always one of the biggest factors to take into consideration on demonstrations. Many of the airfields where the actual demonstrations took place were basic at best, so the likelihood of there being usable fuel was minimal. Others, which in theory had fuel, could run out without there being any sign of replenishment, so it was always worth checking beforehand and, if necessary, carrying extra fuel or picking up extra fuel en route.

On most ferry and demonstration flights, an engineer would be aboard. They would supervise fuelling and check the aircraft for any defects during turnarounds. The engineer would also carry the carnets (fuel cards) to pay for the fuel. On one stopover on an outbound trip through Reykjavik, the engineer was taken ill and was admitted to hospital. It was nothing serious, but he was unable to re-join the flight. This was not a major problem until the fuel had to be paid for in Narsarsuaq, at which time it was discovered that the carnet was still in the possession of the engineer. The chief test pilot paid with his American Express card, confident in the knowledge that he would be reimbursed on his return to the UK. When he arrived home two weeks later, he found a gold American Express card waiting for him!

It is always good to see another 748. The crew of G-BDVH admire an earlier version of the aircraft during a stopover in Sept-Îles, Quebec. (Author)

Chapter 1

Europe

Dan-Air – UK

During the 1980s, one of the best-known names in the airline business in Europe was Dan-Air. With its scheduled routes and holiday charters, its aircraft were to be seen at almost every major airport in Europe. It was also one of the largest operators of the 748, with no less than 21 passing through its hands during the life of the airline. They were mostly used on passenger services, but there was always cargo work to be had as well. One of its most interesting contracts came from the nuclear industry. Dan-Air had won a contract to carry nuclear fuel for British Nuclear Fuels from its facility at Sellafield to Dounreay, on the very north coast of mainland Scotland. Because, for obvious reasons, the routing would not allow the flight over land, the flight-planned route would be from the airfield at Walney Island, near Barrow-in-Furness, up the Irish Sea, west of the Hebrides, and then around the top of the mainland to Dounreay.

For this, they required an LFD, which was normally fitted in the factory as an optional extra. Dan-Air had never bought their 748s direct from the factory and there were none with an LFD available on the used market at the time. There was only one solution: buy a used aircraft and fit a door. The aircraft chosen for the job was G-BIUV, which had previously worn the colours of Polynesian Airlines as 5W-FAN, and spent nine years with the airline. Having found a suitable aircraft, Dan-Air then asked BAe if it could fit the door. Aircraft manufacturers do not normally like doing third-party conversion work, so the figure quoted for the work was sufficiently high for Dan-Air to go away for a rethink. A compromise was eventually reached, whereby BAe supplied the door and the drawings, and Dan-Air did the work at the 748 maintenance base at Manchester Airport. However, the contract did not materialise, and the aircraft was used on Dan-Air's normal services instead. In 1992, however, it became an electoral platform for the Liberal Party, flying around the UK with 'Liberal Democrats' and 'My Vote' emblazoned on the fuselage, before being sold to Emerald Airways shortly afterwards.

G-BCDZ on finals at Farnborough, during a display in 1978. (Gerry Manning)

Emerald Airways – UK

Emerald also had a large 748 fleet and, like Dan-Air, all were obtained from previous operators, including six from Dan-Air. Emerald operated both contracted and ad hoc charters, having been established at Southend Airport in 1987. The company was renamed Emerald Airways in 1992, as a tribute to the amount of work that it carried out across the Irish Sea. There was an incident on 8 March 2006, when G-BVOV overran the runway at Guernsey. It was eventually repaired and returned to service, but, as the result of an inquiry into the incident, the airline's operating certificate was withdrawn by the UK Civil Aviation Authority, the fleet was grounded, and Emerald ceased operating on 4 May 2006. The aircraft then spent some time at Blackpool, Emerald's engineering base, where it was eventually dismantled before being taken to Capernwray Diving Centre in Lancashire, where, in March 2010, it was reassembled and sunk to become an artificial reef for scuba divers.

During its period of operation, Emerald operated a total of 28 748s.

DLT – Germany

Originally formed as Ostfriesische Lufttaxi in 1958, DLT was renamed in 1974, and began a co-operation agreement with Lufthansa in 1978, operating short-haul international services from its base in Cologne. The company bought a total of six new 748 2B Series, with the first three aircraft being delivered between March and July 1981 and leased two other aircraft. The aircraft were particularly striking because, at one point in their lives, they carried an all-red colour scheme, known within Germany as the 'Red Barons'. However, they later carried a similar scheme to that of Lufthansa, with a dark blue cheat line and white roof. DLT's co-operation agreement with Lufthansa meant that they were seen all over Europe, as their principal task was to open new routes for the parent company. The 748s were taken out of service during 1988, and in March 1992, the airline was renamed Lufthansa CityLine.

Howard Hughes

Probably the most unusual sale of a 748 was the one to Howard Hughes. Although well-known at the time, not least for his ownership of Trans World Airlines and Hughes Air West, it was equally well-known that he was very much a recluse. Just before Christmas in 1972, he had arrived at Gatwick and was

G-AYYG was originally the Hawker Siddeley demonstrator, which was later sold to Howard Hughes, although it retained the original colour scheme during that time. (Ken Haynes)

staying in London. Contact was made with the contracts department at Woodford and the contract manager and chief test pilot were asked to come to London for a meeting. Hughes used an intermediary for most of his meetings, and via the intermediary it was determined that Hughes was interested in the 748. Hughes had done his homework and made it clear that although the aircraft was at Woodford, he wanted to fly from Hatfield. He also wanted to have a number of test flights before deciding whether to buy it. The demonstrator at the time was G-AYYG, a Series 2A aircraft. Hughes had insisted on having Tony Blackman, the chief test pilot at the time, as the pilot in command. Hughes wanted the aircraft to be positioned to Hatfield and be at his disposal, along with engineers. He would not give a definite day or time for the flight but was prepared to pay for the aircraft to be available at his whim.

The next task was to arrange for Hughes to arrive at Hatfield in total secrecy. At the time, there was a back way into Hatfield, via which they could enter the hangar. A date was finally agreed, and Hughes was smuggled out of his five-star hotel in central London in the service lift and into a chauffeur-driven car. He duly arrived at Hatfield and met up with the Woodford people in a local hotel car park. The first of several test flights took place, all in the utmost secrecy, and not without some difficulty. Finally, Hughes agreed to buy the demonstrator. It was registered in November 1973, not to Hughes directly, of course, but to a company called Dakota and South Bend Securities Company Ltd, based in London. The aircraft was never used by him. Apart from regular maintenance and periodic engine runs, the aircraft rarely left the hangar at Woodford. Following the death of Hughes in 1976, the aircraft was transferred back to Hawker Siddeley, and soon afterwards was sold to Mount Cook Airlines in New Zealand.

Ryanair – Ireland

Every successful enterprise begins in a small way, and Ryanair is no exception. Tony Ryan, a former director of Aer Lingus, believed that the air fares between the UK and Ireland were too high and out of the reach of many Irish people working in the UK, especially those living in the southeast of England who could not afford the ticket price, and were faced with a long train journey, followed by a ferry trip to reach their homeland. Ryan had founded Guinness Peat Aviation (GPA), which became the world's biggest aircraft lessor, but, not content with that, he began to explore how he could offer cheap flights across the Irish Sea. He came up with the idea of running a coach service from central London to Luton Airport, which would then connect with a flight to Dublin. In 1986, he launched the service using two Series 1A 748s, one ex-Dan-Air and the other from Air Condal, which fortuitously had been stored at Shannon, the headquarters of GPA. The flights, which ran four times a day, quickly became very popular, and by the end of that year were being operated by ROMBAC 1-11s. The 748s were then used on the service from Luton to the newly opened airport at Knock, in the northwest of Ireland, and for ad hoc charter work. As the airline continued its rapid growth, both aircraft had been disposed of by the end of 1988. The rest of the Ryanair story is history, with the 748 yet again playing a major part in an airline's initial development.

SATA – the Azores

The Azores are a group of nine islands that lie 1,000 miles (1,600km) off the west coast of Portugal. The autonomous government of the Azores called for the setting up of an airline to provide a link between the islands, all of which have an airport. SATA was originally formed as a private company in 1947, but on 17 October 1987, the regional government took over the airline and it was renamed SATA Air Açores. The airline is completely self-contained and carries out all maintenance and crew training at its base in Ponta Delgada, the largest city in the archipelago.

SATA's relationship with the 748 began in 1969, with the lease of a Series 2A leased from Hawker Siddeley for a two-month period. This was followed by the lease of two Series 2s from Autair the

G-AZSU wore a number of different colours during its life. A Series 2 model, it operated with Aberdeen Airways between 1990 and 1992. (Gerry Manning)

following year. Various other 748 leases followed, culminating in the purchase of two new Series 2As, which were delivered in 1970 and 1973. A third aircraft followed in 1980. The Azores are a holiday destination and there was a considerable increase in traffic during the summer months, when additional aircraft were leased in from other operators, such as Mount Cook, Dan-Air and Air Madagascar.

In 1987, SATA upgraded the fleet by ordering two Series 2Bs, with the original 2As being taken in part-exchange by BAe. These operated until 1992, when they were returned to BAe, following the delivery of three new ATPs. Including the lease aircraft, SATA operated 16 different 748s. From being an inter-island carrier, SATA has grown significantly and has been re-branded as Azores Airlines, with routes to North America and Europe.

Olympic Airways – Greece

Olympic Airways had always been something of a problem child for the Greek government. It was important for Greece to have a national airline, but the poor Greek economy and the huge overheads meant that the airline never made a profit. In July 1956, the government sold the airline to the Greek shipowner Aristotle Onassis. He had amassed his wealth by operating what had become the world's largest privately owned fleet of oil tankers. Under the ownership of Onassis, the airline acquired a reputation for lavish style. First-class passengers ate with gold cutlery whilst listening to a pianist and being served by cabin staff wearing uniforms designed by Pierre Cardin.

This was fine for the longer-haul routes, but air services to the many islands were still sporadic and Olympic was asked to address the problem. Between June and October 1969, the Series 2A demonstrator (G-AVRR) was leased to Olympic to assess the viability of regular services to the larger islands. The demonstration was successful, and an order was placed by Olympic for the purchase of eight aircraft. At the time, Onassis was negotiating with the Japanese for the purchase of eight supertankers. The Japanese, fully aware that the NAMC YS-11 was achieving very few export sales, saw an opportunity and told Onassis that for each supertanker he bought, they would give him a YS-11 free of charge. Onassis was a businessman, and it was obviously an opportunity too good to ignore, so the YS-11s were ordered instead and delivered during 1970. The death of Onassis' son, Alexander, in a plane crash in January 1973 had a significant effect on Onassis, and a few months later he sold all his shares back to the

G-BNJK sits in a hangar at Cranfield, whilst undergoing its conversion to a turbine tanker for Macavia Ltd. (Gerry Manning)

Greek government. Onassis died in 1975. Meanwhile, the YS-11s were suffering reliability problems in Olympic service and by 1980, all the remaining aircraft had been transferred to the Hellenic Air Force.

West Air Sweden

With bases in both Malmö and Lidköping, West Air Sweden was set up to handle cargo on behalf of the major courier companies. Additionally, it operated ad hoc charter services. It is also contracted to operate mail flights on behalf of the Swedish Post Office and the Royal Mail in the UK.

Beginning originally as an air taxi operator in 1955, the company went through various changes until it was named West Air Sweden in 1992, and in May 1997 it became an all-cargo airline. In 2002, it was reorganised and became West Air Europe Aktiebolag (AB). Following this, West Air won a contract with the Norwegian postal service, thus adding significant capacity to West Air. In 2008, West Air acquired Atlantic Airlines, a UK-based cargo carrier. The merger was not completed until late in 2011, by which time both carriers were trading as West Atlantic. The parent company, West Air Europe AB, was renamed West Atlantic AB.

The airline chose the 748 to expand its operations and went into the used market, beginning with the four former DFS (German air traffic control) aircraft in 1995. These had originally been delivered as Series 2s but were modified to Series 2As. Further aircraft followed, including two Series 2s from the RAAF in March 1999. These aircraft were also converted to Series 2As, together with a further aircraft previously owned by Fred Olsen. The aircraft all had APUs fitted, but these were deemed as being unnecessary weight and subsequently removed. All the aircraft were completely stripped out and fitted with LFDs. Additionally, an Air Inuit aircraft, C-FDOX, was leased between March 1999 and January 2000 to provide additional capacity. As the 748s gradually ran out of life, they were sold on, and ATPs, also sourced from the used market, began to be introduced. All were converted to have LFDs and West Atlantic is now the world's largest operator of the ATP.

The question has often been asked why the registration G-AVRO was applied to a Britannia Airways Boeing 737-200 rather than a 748, when, at the time of application, it would have been available. The explanation is simple. The possibility of using the registration was pointed out to the directors at Woodford, but they considered that at the time (1967), the company was now known as Hawker Siddeley, thus it would no longer be appropriate to use that registration. As a result, the aircraft that was to be used as the next demonstrator, with construction number 1635, became G-AVRR.

G-BIUV, originally a Series 2A, was converted to have an LFD fitted. It visited RAF Valley during the election campaign of 1992. (Andy Hutchings)

CS-TAO, a Series 2A in the original SATA colours, takes a break between flights on the island of Horta. (Author)

Skyways Series 2 G-AXVG is seen here at the old terminal at Liverpool's Speke Airport in 1970. It later wore Dan-Air colours, following its takeover of Skyways. (Bob O'Brien Collection)

Omega Express was owned by Securicor, and the 748s were used principally for moving mail around the UK. G-OSOE was formerly G-AYYG, the Hawker Siddeley Aviation demonstrator. (Bob O'Brien Collection)

British Airways Highlands Division operated a fleet of 748s, both around Scotland and as far south as Manchester. (Bob O'Brien Collection)

XS 790 was originally based at RAF Benson and served with The Queen's Flight for 25 years. (Bob O'Brien Collection)

Seen here at an unusually quiet Manchester Airport, G-HDBB, a Series 2B of British Airways Highlands Division, was delivered in 1984. (Bob O'Brien Collection)

Channel Airways' distinctive gold colour scheme was seen throughout the UK during its 11 years of operation. (Bob O'Brien Collection)

This Maersk Air Series 2A did not stay long with the airline. It was formerly owned by LAN-Chile and served with the Danish carrier for just a year. (Bob O'Brien Collection)

Linhas Aéreas Regionais was a second-level carrier in Portugal, operating domestic and a few international flights. (Bob O'Brien Collection)

BKS operated this Series 2 between 1965 and 1966. Here, it is seen between flights at Leeds Bradford Airport. (Lloyd P Robinson)

The original terminal building at East Midlands Airport is the background for Channel Airways Series 2, G-ATEH. (Brian Tonge)

G-BOHZ began life as D-AHSB with DLT, but the Series 2B is seen here at Southend, awaiting a new customer. (Lloyd P Robinson)

This 2007 photograph was taken at Blackpool Airport, showing nine 748s at Emerald's maintenance base. (Lloyd P Robinson)

Series 1 G-BEJD, seen here, looking rather bedraggled at Emerald's Blackpool maintenance base. (Lloyd P Robinson)

A former Mount Cook Series 2 undergoes some line maintenance at Blackpool. (Lloyd P Robinson)

This aircraft wore many different colour schemes during its life. It was registered in Mexico, the Philippines, Ghana, Denmark, Zambia and, ultimately, Canada. (David R Lawrence)

Former Aerolíneas Argentinas and Dan-Air Series 1, G-BEJD is being preserved at the site of the old airport at Speke, Liverpool. (Lloyd P Robinson)

Autair Series 2 G-ATMJ seen here at Speke Airport, Liverpool. It carried many different colours during its life. (Bob O'Brien Collection)

G-AVRR began its life as a demonstrator aircraft in 1967 and was leased to a number of different operators. (David R Lawrence)

Originally delivered as a Series 2 in 1969, this aircraft was later modified to a Series 2A and used as an airfield calibrator. (David R Lawrence)

This aircraft, a Series 2, was used as a certification aircraft for the Dart 8 engines supplied for the Argosy. (David R Lawrence)

Left: As it says on the trolley, this is the forward cockpit section of G-ORAL, still to be seen at the Speke Aerodrome Heritage Group. It was originally supplied to TTAS as 9Y-TFS. (Lloyd P Robinson)

Below: Class B registration G-11-9 was allocated to three different aircraft. This Series 2A became F-BUTR with Rousseau Aviation in France. (David R Lawrence)

The original Dan-Air colour scheme is evident on this Air Condal Series 1, the only 748 to appear on the Spanish register. The aircraft was based in Palma de Mallorca. (Buckerbook.com)

Right: Not a common sight, this is what most aircraft look like before the colour scheme is applied. The BAe demonstrator, G-BGJV, is seen here outside the flight sheds at Woodford. (Shaun Connor)

Below: EI-BSE, one of the first aircraft to be operated by Ryanair, awaits its next departure at Luton in 1988. (Gerry Manning)

Chapter 2
Africa

The 748 was designed with Africa in mind. Not only was it quite capable of taking off from unprepared strips, but many of the countries in East Africa have a lot of high ground. This is a problem for aircraft engines, because the combination of thin and hot air significantly reduces the power of the engines. This means that the lifting power of the aircraft is reduced, which, in turn, means that its maximum take-off weight must be reduced, meaning less seats can be sold. One way to assist with this is to cool the engines when they are at maximum power by the injection of a substance called water methanol into the combustion chamber, which has the effect of lowering the temperature whilst, at the same time, increasing the power output. This means that at some of the higher altitude airports, such as Nairobi, Entebbe, Blantyre, and Johannesburg, the aircraft could usually operate to its maximum potential.

Above: Carrying both its real and its class 'B' registration, Series 2B G-11-10, alias TJ-CCF, is in the final preparation stage at Woodford before delivery. (Shaun Connor)

Left: The appropriately registered Series 2B is seen here at Manchester Airport. It was an unannounced sale to what was then Upper Volta, now Burkina Faso. (Shaun Connor)

Africa

One of the three Series 2A aircraft, leased by Ghana Airways, sits outside the flight sheds at Woodford. (David R Lawrence)

G-ATAM wears a Ghana Airways scheme, as it is prepared for a lease in 1969. It became 9G-ABV during the lease. (Bob O'Brien Collection)

Undergoing an engine run before the final titles are applied, this Series 2A is almost ready to join its stablemate at Air Malawi. (David R Lawrence)

Air Malawi
Based in Malawi's capital, Blantyre, the airline took delivery of two 748 2A Series in December 1969 and January 1970. These were used initially on domestic services, with additional routes to the neighbouring countries of Mozambique, Zambia, and Zimbabwe. Initially, the colour scheme was quite bland, but later service saw the aircraft with bright red tailfins and the distinctive vector logo, as used on Air Malawi's VC-10 and Boeing 747SP.

Williamson Diamonds Ltd – Tanzania
One of the more unusual operators of the 748 was a mining company based in Tanzania. It had previously owned two DC-3s and a de Havilland Dove. Its operations were based near the site of a mine at an airstrip called Mwadui, which is situated 4,000ft (1,200m) above sea level, and is a gravel strip with a single runway 4,600ft (1,400m) long, located about 450 miles (725km) northwest of the former capital, Dar es Salaam. The 748 was, thus, perfectly fulfilling its role as a DC-3 replacement.

The aircraft was used to transport both passengers and cargo and had been fitted with an LFD. Owing to the remoteness of the mine operation, it was required to transport both personnel and equipment from both Dar es Salaam and Nairobi. The company took delivery of 5H-WDL in April 1976 and it stayed in service until it was sold to South Africa in 1996, and then later to South Sudan, where it was written off following a runway excursion in March 2006 as 5Y-TCA.

Guinea-Bissau
One of the lesser-known countries of Africa, the former Portuguese colony of Guinea-Bissau lies between Senegal and Guinea on the west coast of the continent. Following its declaration of independence from Portugal in 1974, a 748 Series 2A was ordered to operate for Linhas Aéreas da Guiné-Bissau. The aircraft, J5-GAT, named 'Madina de Boie' after the region in which the independence documents were signed, was delivered in December 1978, and was quickly put into operation on the airline's route network. Its routes were to neighbouring countries – Senegal, Cape Verde, the Gambia, and Guinea – and a domestic flight to Bubaque, a grass-strip airfield next to the main town on a group of islands off the coast. At the time, this was the biggest aircraft in its fleet.

Guinea-Bissau bought a single Series 2A to operate to the nearby countries of Senegal, Zambia, and Cape Verde. It also visited the Canary Islands. (Bob O'Brien Collection)

When an F-27, one of three the airline operated, crashed in Burkina Faso in August 1991, it was discovered that the three crew members were Palestinian. This brought to light the role of the Palestine Liberation Organisation (PLO) in the operation of the airline since the mid-1980s. It was alleged that the PLO had supplied the airline with the aircraft and crews. In 1989, the name of the airline was changed to Air Bissau and the 748 was repainted in the new colours. Air Bissau ceased operating in 1998 and the aircraft was sold to West Air Sweden, where it had an LFD conversion.

TACV – Cabo Verde

Cape Verde, as it is better known, is a group of ten islands off the west coast of Africa. Transportes Aéreos Cabo Verde (TACV) began life in 1958 but had to suspend operations in 1967 owing to a shortage of aircraft. In 1975, following independence from Portugal, TAP agreed to provide technical

TACV aircraft normally carried Portuguese overseas (CR) registrations until independence, but this Series 2A was sold to an American company. (Lloyd P Robinson)

assistance to restart operations. Prior to this, in 1974, TACV had ordered two 748 Series 2A to operate on its domestic services, connecting a number of the main islands in the archipelago. These were the only routes operated by the airline until 1984. To the rear of the blue wing tail logo are seven lines, each of which represents an island served by the airline. Initially, the registrations allocated reflected the fact that the nation was still under the control of Portugal, and the colonial registrations of CR-CAV and CR-CAX, respectively, were allocated to them. However, it was later discovered that CR-CAX had been allocated to a DHC Twin Otter and the registration was changed to CR-CAW. In November 1984, both registrations were changed to a 'D4-' prefix, following the reallocation by International Civil Aviation Organization (ICAO).

Transkei Airways Corporation
Transkei was an unrecognised state within the south-eastern region of South Africa until 1994. It was an area that operated nominally as an independent nation, set aside for black South Africans of Xhosa descent, and was also the birthplace of Nelson Mandela. As such, negotiations for the sale of an aircraft into the region were delicate. Apartheid was still being practised in South Africa when negotiations began, but in early 1979, a deal was concluded and a Series 2A, ZS-XGE, was delivered in August 1979 and used primarily on a service between Johannesburg and Umtata (now renamed Mthatha), the regional capital. At the time of operation, the runways were grass with the airport at an elevation of 2,500ft (760m) above sea level – ideal operating conditions for a 748. The airport has since been considerably improved. The aircraft was disposed of in 1993, following the interim lease of a Convair 580. The airline was renamed Eastern Air in 1995.

Zambian Air Force
A Series 2 aircraft was delivered to the Zambian Air Force in June 1967. This was sold and fitted as a VIP aircraft for President Kaunda and was allocated the serial number AF 601. However, the aircraft, whilst being flown by a crew seconded from the Royal Air Force, crashed in Lusaka a little more than two years later. The president was not on board.

A replacement aircraft was ordered and delivered in February 1971. This one was a Series 2A version and was allocated the serial number AF 602. There were reports at the time that this had also crashed in 1990, but the aircraft concerned was, in fact, a DHC-5 Buffalo. Unusually at that time, both aircraft were fitted with an APU, which was housed in a fairing above the starboard engine. The APU fitment had two advantages: firstly, to keep the cabin cool during the heat of the Zambian day and, secondly, to provide electrical power at airports where none would otherwise be available.

This aircraft has lasted considerably longer than its predecessor and was seen at Rand Airport near Johannesburg in 2014, but with parts missing.

Air Madagascar
Hollywood made this African island famous with DreamWorks' 2005 movie. Prior to that, it was virtually unknown, yet in area terms, it is larger than Spain. Air Madagascar began life in 1947 and was renamed Madair in April 1961 after becoming the flag carrier, but the name was changed back to Air Madagascar in October 1962 after the negative connotations of the name were realised.

By 1972, there were seven DHC-6 Twin Otters in the fleet, but the airline wanted a larger aircraft. The aircraft in prime position to replace them was the DHC Dash 7, primarily because of its short take-off and landing (STOL) capabilities on Madagascar's short fields. A thorough evaluation took place, together with demonstrations by all the contenders, including the F-27. Fokker had offered the F-27 and used the local media to present some negative perceptions of the 748. Despite this, the

Air Madagascar ordered four new Series 2Bs. This example was equipped with an LFD, seen here at the capital, Antananarivo. (Bob O'Brien Collection)

748 won the contest, helped enormously by its ability over several days to reliably fly the ten-sector Twin Otter schedule.

Air Madagascar ordered three 748s; two were Series 2B with LFDs. The third, also a 2B, was in VIP configuration and used for the Presidential Flight. The first two were delivered in 1980, whilst the third aircraft was delivered in April 1981 and used from time to time on domestic services. All three 748s flew on domestic routes within Madagascar. The airline-configured aircraft were with the carrier until 1989, when they were sold to Horizon Airlines in Australia.

Air Liberia

Air Liberia bought a Series 2A, which was delivered in February 1978. However, the route to its purchase was far from smooth. The airline had previously operated Islanders, Trislanders and a DC-3 and wanted a larger and more modern aircraft to operate on its domestic routes.

As ever, there was competition between Woodford and Fokker for the deal, and it was purely a twist of fate that ensured that Woodford won the deal. Negotiations were well under way when the vice president died suddenly. As a result, arrangements were made, as per his dying wish, to convey his body to his hometown of Sinoe, in the south of the country. The casket was huge and very heavy, and the airfield at Sinoe was unpaved; these two situations weighed against the possibility of the F-27 being able to carry out the operation. Hawker Siddeley offered its demonstrator with the LFD to perform the task, and the 748 was equal to it. Nevertheless, the cabinet was split over which aircraft to buy; the deciding vote was cast by the president himself in favour of the 748, because of its role in conveying the vice president respectfully to his resting place.

The aircraft was used principally on domestic routes but was written off in April 1983, after losing an engine during take-off from Khartoum, Sudan.

Air Gabon

The equatorial country of Gabon, located on the west coast of Africa, was one of many countries in the region to buy the 748. The lease of the first 748 to what was formerly called Société Nationale

Air Gabon operated three Series 2s. This aircraft crashed shortly after taking off from Libreville on 8 June 2004. (Lloyd P Robinson)

Transgabon took place in 1971, when G-AVRR, a Series 2A demonstrator, was leased to the airline in October of that year. A year later, it formally bought the aircraft, which became TR-LQJ. A second aircraft, this time a Series 2, G-ATAM, also an ex-demonstrator, was delivered in October 1972 and re-registered as TR-LQY. At the time, the airline was operating two YS-11s from Air Afrique, based in the Ivory Coast capital of Abidjan, but they had proved unreliable and the carrier needed a more dependable aircraft. The 748s were used mainly on domestic routes, with a twice-monthly schedule to Lomé (Togo) on behalf of Air Afrique.

On 3 November 1971, one of the YS-11s was unserviceable, and the 748 was called in to replace it. This was particularly important, as the flight was scheduled to operate from the seaport of Port Gentil to Libreville to connect with the Air Afrique direct flight to Paris. In fact, the 748 should have been flying to Lastoursville in the centre of the country, but, after dropping off the passengers in Libreville, it picked up its original schedule and eventually arrived back at Libreville on schedule. This was one of a number of incidents that had convinced the airline to buy the 748. Both aircraft were ultimately sold to Canada after being replaced by Boeing 737-200s. In March 1976, TR-LQJ was sold to Eastern Provincial Airways, with TR-LQY following the same route to Austin Airways in May of the same year. In mid-1974, the name of the airline was changed to the simpler Air Gabon, and in 1977, the carrier withdrew from the Air Afrique consortium. Having operated an astonishing 31 different types of aircraft, the airline was declared bankrupt in 2006.

South Africa
No fewer than 26 748s were registered in South Africa, although the picture is somewhat confusing.

South African Airways
South African Airways (SAA) operated five 748s. Three Series 2A aircraft were ordered, one of which was then immediately leased to Botswana Airways Corporation as A2-ZFT. The aircraft were delivered

in early 1971. Prior to this, two lease aircraft, one being G-ATAM, had been provided during 1970 in order for route-proving trials to be carried out. This was painted in full SAA colours and re-registered as ZS-HSA. The second aircraft was a Series 2A, originally registered as G-AVRR, but as with the above aircraft, it was painted in full SAA colours and re-registered as ZS-HSI. They were principally used on routes from Johannesburg to neighbouring countries such as Botswana, Lesotho, Namibia, and Mozambique. All three of the newly purchased aircraft were sold to Canada in 1983.

Air Cape

The airline's route network was integrated with that of SAA, and it would often fly its routes as a full-service carrier. G-AVRR, which had been previously leased to SAA as a demonstrator, flew its schedules for two weeks in December 1969 as part of a route evaluation, but it was not until 1974 when the distinctive colours of Air Cape were seen on a Series 2A, which had been bought from Rousseau Aviation of France and registered as ZS-JAY. The airline was taken over by Safair (Freighters) Ltd in May 1988 and renamed Safair Lines. This company had two Convair 580s, and the 748 was disposed of later that year to a company called Kel Air in France.

Aerospace Express

This company went into the used aircraft market to buy the last 748 to be built, which had originally been supplied to Makung Airlines of Taiwan. The aircraft was then sold on to Necon Air in Nepal and was bought by the South African company in 2001 and registered as ZS-AGB. The aircraft was then leased to Lion Air of Sri Lanka and later returned to South Africa in 2004, following which it does not appear to have done any flying, apart from a short lease to Comores Aviation. The aircraft lay derelict at Johannesburg's Oliver Tambo Airport for several years, before being broken up in 2012.

What is curious about the registration though, is that it appeared on an aircraft in Thailand, despite never leaving South Africa. The Thai aircraft had been supplied to Thai Airways as HS-THH in 1972. Following an accident in 1987, the aircraft was dismantled and taken to a town south of the resort of Pattaya and had Lion Air titles applied, together with the registration ZS-AGB. It was then moved to another resort on the western coast of Thailand and now sits in a garden of flowers, with the interior converted into a double bedroom. Quite how and why it acquired this registration when it never left the country is anyone's guess.

Executive Aerospace

Originally set up in 1984 and based in Durban, the company moved to Johannesburg in 1999. It was not an airline as such, but a tour operator that also offered charters. In addition, it bought and leased out used aircraft to other operators, both in Africa and Asia. The company also converted two aircraft into freighters, to be used for work in Africa with the Red Cross and United Nations. A total of eight aircraft, including Series 2, 2A and 2B, were operated during the lifetime of the company. Despite regular leasing work, the company failed financially and was wound up by the High Court of Durban in 2008.

Intensive Air

The Johannesburg-based company operated three 748s, one an LFD ex-Williamson Diamonds, one a former Bahamasair Series 2A, and one a further 2A, formerly owned by Transkei Airways Corporation. The aircraft were leased out to other operators such as Air Botswana and Air Malawi and operated a scheduled service from Johannesburg to Margate, a beach resort on the KwaZulu-Natal coast. The former Bahamasair aircraft, registered ZS-XGY, was involved in a bizarre accident on 29 May 1998.

Avro 748

An inaugural flight from Madrid with an Iberia A340, EC-GJT, had arrived at Johannesburg on the morning of 20 May, following an absence from the route of more than ten years. Once the arrival ceremonies had taken place, the aircraft was towed to a remote stand to await the evening return to Madrid. Later in the day, ZS-XGY was taxiing behind the A340 when, following a total hydraulic failure, there was a collision between the two aircraft. The propeller on the No.1 engine (port side) struck the rear fuselage of the A340, and the 748s vertical stabiliser was then severely damaged as the aircraft became wedged under the rear fuselage of the A340. Both aircraft suffered major damage, but both were subsequently repaired and returned to service. The company ceased operating in April 2002.

Left: Stars Away Aviation was based in Cape Town and operated four 748s between 2006 and 2012. (Lloyd P Robinson)

Below: Parked in a remote corner of Durban's former international airport is ZS-DBM in another colour scheme. (Lloyd P Robinson)

This Series 2A, almost certainly ZS-XGY, is parked at Oliver Tambo Airport, Johannesburg, and is clearly being used for spares. (Lloyd P Robinson)

Above: ZS-AGB is undergoing maintenance at Oliver Tambo Airport, Johannesburg. This was the last Series 2B to be delivered. (Lloyd P Robinson)

Right: Once with the Royal Air Force, this Series 2 is parked at Lanseria Airport, South Africa. (Lloyd P Robinson)

Zone 4 Uganda

This Entebbe-based cargo operator was founded in 2010 to supply humanitarian and relief operations in East and Central Africa. Principal among their services is the carriage of perishable goods from Entebbe to South Sudan in co-operation with the United Nations Mission in South Sudan (UNMISS).

The company operates a former Lufthansa Boeing 727 in full cargo configuration and two 748s, a Series 2A and a Series 2B, both with large freight doors. The Series 2A was formerly 9N-ACP of Necon Air of Nepal, via Executive Air of South Africa. The Series 2B previously wore the colours of DLT, as D-AHSA, and British Airways, as G-BOHY, but more recently carried the registration 5Y-CBI.

Once again, the 748 was chosen for its ability to operate from unpaved strips, which form the majority of airfields in South Sudan. In addition, Zone 4 also provides fuel transport and medevac services to support the local mining operations.

Both aircraft are now registered in Tajikistan, the Series 2A as EY-638 and the 2B as EY-639.

Series 2B EY-639 sits in a parking area at Bentiu airfield in South Sudan. The 748s provide a lifeline to many remote parts of the country, which is approximately the same size as France. (Mads Oyen)

This photo clearly shows the striking Zone 4 colour scheme. Formerly 5Y-CBI, this aircraft, and its sister ship, EY-638, are still working in South Sudan and both are operated by Zone 4 International, based in Entebbe, Uganda. It is seen here in April 2021 in South Sudan. (Mads Oyen)

The first of the Air Madagascar order to be delivered. The LFD was fitted to both aircraft delivered to the airline. (Bob O'Brien Collection)

Originally owned by German carrier DLT, this Series 2B, seen here in Durban, wore several colour schemes prior to this one. (Bob O'Brien Collection)

Chapter 3
Middle East and Asia

Hindustan Aeronautics Ltd (HAL) – India

From the earliest days of the 748, India had shown a considerable amount of interest in the aircraft. The Indian Air Force had operated a fleet of 33 DC-3s and a replacement was required, whilst Indian Airlines also operated a fleet of more than 20 DC-3s.

Following an extensive tour of the facilities at Chadderton and Woodford, the Indian Ministry of Defence signed an agreement in July 1959 to produce the aircraft under licence in India. The agreement called for kits to be supplied from Manchester and final assembly to take place at the Indian Air Force base at Kanpur, northern India. One year later, the first kit was flown out from Woodford, together with a team of engineers, jigs, and tooling. The first flight of a Kanpur-assembled aircraft, carrying the serial number BH 572, followed in November 1961. This was a Series 1 aircraft.

The aircraft built in India differed slightly from their British-built counterparts in that all were fitted with an LFD, together with a strengthened fuselage floor, to enable them to carry cargo. In concert with this, the maximum take-off weight was also increased.

The production at Kanpur was much slower than at Manchester and it was March 1963 before the first production aircraft took to the skies. However, there was some disappointment with the specifications of the Series 1 and, following a visit by what had now become the Series 2 demonstrator, G-ARAY, the Indian government decided that only four Series 1 aircraft would be produced, and that any future aircraft would be Series 2s. As part of this decision, Hindustan Aeronautics Ltd (HAL) took over the Kanpur plant. New production targets were set, and the aircraft was to become known as the HAL 748. This did not entirely solve the problem, however, and by 1965, only four aircraft had been test-flown. The programme was in danger of being wound up when Indian Airlines Corporation (IAC) placed an order in December 1965 for 15 aircraft as replacements for their DC-3s. In February 1966, the first of these was test-flown. Registered as VT-DUO, it was later flown to Woodford for fitting out to a commercial standard. It did not return to India until the following year, when it was officially handed over to IAC on 22 June 1967.

Meanwhile, the production rate at Kanpur had not improved and IAC was not prepared to go on waiting for its aircraft. As a result, it ordered a batch of F-27s. Even when the production rates improved during the late 1960s, it was not the end of HAL's problems. IAC had placed an order for ten further aircraft, but of these, only three were accepted. IAC refused the others on the basis that modifications suggested by HAL would increase the weight of the aircraft and, therefore, the operating costs. These aircraft were placed into storage but were later reallocated for work with the Air Force, who took three of them and then various government agencies took another three, with the final aircraft going to the Indian Border Security Force in 1982.

The slow production rate and the problems with the IAC order meant that the whole operation was becoming something of a scandal, and a government-led team was set up to investigate the situation. Slowly but surely, the production rate and build quality improved, and the Indian Air Force ordered more aircraft, primarily for VIP and training roles. By 1975, the Air Force had received 45 aircraft in total. The Air Force put the aircraft to innovative uses, one of which was the seconding of an aircraft to the Defence Research and Development Organisation (DRDO), who fitted an AWACS-style rotodome to the roof of the aircraft. This is quite possibly the most unusual use to which a 748 airframe has been put. The chosen aircraft, which carried the serial H-2175, was flown to the DRDO specialist centre

In poor condition, but still largely intact, Hindustan-built VT-EFR was a flight inspection aircraft. It was parked at Indira Ghandi Airport, Delhi. (Lloyd P Robinson)

in Bangalore after production, in order for the rotodome to be fitted. Unfortunately, the programme was later abandoned. In an accident on 11 January 1999, it appears, from the fact that the rotodome was discovered some 1.2 miles (2km) from the site of the accident at Arakkonam Naval Air Station in eastern India, that it had become detached from the fuselage and in the process had damaged the flying surfaces, bringing down the aircraft.

The Royal Brunei Malay Regiment was an unusual purchaser of the 748. This Series 2A, AMDB -110, is seen taxiing at Woodford. (David R Lawrence)

Although built by Hindustan Aeronautics, this aircraft was flown to Woodford for painting and interior finishing. (David R Lawrence)

Production of the 748 finally ended in 1984, with the last example coming off the line after 89 aircraft had been built. The inability of HAL to produce aircraft at the rates originally envisaged, plus its inability to modify the aircraft to full Series 2A standards, as per the British-produced aircraft, meant that the demand for the aircraft had dried up. No HAL-built aircraft were sold outside of India, despite its early attempts to promote the aircraft in Southeast Asia.

Bouraq Indonesia Airlines

Based in Jakarta and flying an extensive domestic network within the Indonesian islands, Bouraq was established in 1970 as a privately owned company by the Sumendap family. The name Bouraq comes from the name of a traditional Muslim flying horse. Bouraq became a major operator of the 748 over a period of 32 years.

Initially, the airline had started up with a single DC-3, but in 1973 it had ordered three new Series 2A 748s, with the last aircraft being delivered in August 1974. It later bought six of the 11 former Varig aircraft during late 1976, and five of the former nine LAN-Chile aircraft during 1978. A further order for six new 2Bs followed, with the first aircraft being built in a batch with LFDs. Subsequently registered

Series 2A PK-MHM receives some engineering attention during a stopover in Jakarta. It was one of two aircraft sold to the Indonesian carrier. (Bob O'Brien Collection)

Series 2B G-BKLD is seen here at the Paris Air Show in 1983, wearing its show number, before delivery to Bouraq. (Bob O'Brien Collection)

PK-IHO, the aircraft was delivered in June 1983 following an appearance in full Bouraq colours at the Paris Air Show. The final aircraft was delivered to Bouraq in May 1983.

As low-cost carriers began to appear in Indonesia, Bouraq found the competition was becoming more intense and it began to lose money. Prolonged financial problems eventually overtook the carrier, and it was shut down in 2005. Only one of the Bouraq fleet left Indonesia, which was a Series 2A sold to Bradley Air Services in Canada, re-registered as C-GTLD and put into service in September 1979.

Makung International Airways – Taiwan

The last two 748s ever built, both Series 2Bs, were sold to Makung Airways in 1988 and 1989. Makung (also known as Magong) is actually an island off the west coast of Taiwan, and the airline was set up in 1988 to connect the principal island with Makung Island, but it was in fact based in Kaohsiung. All the flights the aircraft undertook were necessarily domestic, given Taiwan's fractious relationship with its near neighbour, the People's Republic of China. Makung is used by the Taiwanese as a holiday island.

The airport at Makung originally had a short runway of 3,000ft (914m), enough for the 748 to be able to operate comfortably on a short sector to Kaohsiung, for example. Kaohsiung is Taiwan's second city, a major seaport, and the nearest point on the main island to Makung.

The airline's name was changed to Uni Air on 31 March 1996, after EVA Air took a majority share in the airline. The two 748s left the fleet in December 1997 and were sold to Necon Air, based in Nepal.

Aden Airways

Aden Airways was formed in 1949, as a wholly owned subsidiary of British Overseas Airways Corporation (BOAC). At the time, Aden was a British Crown colony, with regular services by BOAC and was also an important staging post for the Royal Air Force.

In May 1960, an order was placed by Aden Airways for three 748 Series 2s, to be registered VR-AAU, V and W. A fuselage mock-up of a 748 in full Aden Airways colours was displayed at the Farnborough Air Show in September 1960. Following a period of civil unrest, the British withdrew from Aden and the order was cancelled in June 1962, after Aden Airways had entered into a pooled service agreement with East African Airways Corporation, thus bringing about a re-structuring of the network. The aircraft had not been delivered and were reallocated to the Brazilian Air Force order.

It is not entirely surprising that there were not a lot of sales of the 748, or any other regional aircraft, in the Middle East. At that time, aviation was little developed, and populations were much lower than they are today. In the mid-1970s, the population of Saudi Arabia was a little over seven million – today, it exceeds 34 million. It seems almost unbelievable that Dubai, now a major world hub and holiday destination, had a population of just 166,000 in 1975, compared with almost three million today.

Emirates was not founded until 1985 and Etihad not until 2007, so the opportunities to sell any aircraft to a large carrier did not exist. Oman Air operated two F-27s on the 540 miles (869km) domestic service from Muscat to Salalah, but this represented the only regional operation at the time.

The 748 could, however, be seen around the Middle East in the colours of the Royal Air Force at Khormaksar, Aden (21 Sqn), and Muharraq, Bahrain, with the Middle East Communications Squadron (MECS) and 152 Sqn. The biggest base was at Sharjah (then known as the Trucial States, now part of the United Arab Emirates).

The 748's larger cousin, the Andover, was much in evidence in the area, operating for the Royal Air Force, with bases at Sharjah (84 Sqn) and Muharraq, which at the time was home to the MECS.

Air Sinai – Egypt

In 1979, Israel and Egypt signed what has proved to be a historic peace treaty, allowing diplomatic relations to be formalised between what, in the past, had been two warring nations. Within the treaty was a clause that the two countries must maintain an active air route; in other words, there had to be a permanent direct flight between Israel and Egypt.

Air Sinai, founded in 1982, is the result of that clause. Initially, Nefertiti Airlines, also known as Nefertiti Aviation, had first operated the route in 1980 on an ad hoc basis. The flights were considered key to the improvement of Egyptian–Israeli relations, but it was felt that a full scheduled service was required, and it was taken over by Air Sinai. A scheduled service was set up between Cairo and Tel Aviv, using a Boeing 707-331B leased from Trans World Airlines (TWA), which operated between December 1982 and May 1983. The 707 was also used on the Cairo–Copenhagen route and other European flights for EgyptAir, despite being in Air Sinai colours. The short 240-mile (386km) distance between the two cities was ideal for a 748 operation, and in April 1983, Air Sinai agreed a lease for two 748s, a Series 2A and a 2B, both demonstrator aircraft at the time, to operate the route, although the lease was never finalised. Air Sinai took delivery of three F-27-500s from Fokker during 1983 and 1984, with two further aircraft being leased during the same period.

Air Sinai currently uses EgyptAir pilots, aircraft, and flight attendants, operating under a wet-lease agreement, flying under the Air Sinai banner. As such, EgyptAir, for political reasons, was unable to carry out the operation, so a new airline was formed. In 2002, Air Sinai ceased operating as such, although the name continues to exist. Its parent company, EgyptAir, operates the Boeing 737 aircraft, which does not carry any titles, but the aircraft are Egyptian registered.

Ex-Royal Thai Airways, this Royal Thai Air Force Series 2, taxies in at Don Muang Airport, Bangkok, in 1989. (Gerry Manning)

Originally supplied to the Royal Thai Air Force King's Flight, this Series 2 carried the unusual serial 99-999. (Gerry Manning)

Avro 748

A Royal Thai Air Force Series 2, originally supplied to the King's Flight, is preserved at the museum in Bangkok. (Gerry Manning)

Even if the title on the fuselage is unknown to most, there is a strong clue in the mountainous background. The Series 2A was delivered to Nepal Airlines in 1970. (Bob O'Brien Collection)

Middle East and Asia

Merpati was an Indonesian domestic carrier that ordered two Series 2A aircraft. Here, the demonstrator is prepared for the trip to Jakarta. (Bob O'Brien Collection)

Outside the Woodford flight sheds, Series 2 PI-C1023 awaits delivery in February 1969. (David R Lawrence)

False in several respects, the prefix letter 'EX-' was issued to Kyrgyzstan, but with numbers rather than letters, and it is definitely not a 737-900ER! Formerly PK-IHJ, it is seen here in Surabaya, Indonesia. (Russell Legg/Greg Thom)

Another Philippine Airlines aircraft is prepared at Woodford. All in this batch were Series 2s. (David R Lawrence)

This Thai Airways Series 2 example carried the most basic of colour schemes when it left Woodford. (David R Lawrence)

Originally supplied to British Airways, this Series 2B found its way to Sri Lanka via Nepal and Australia. Its service life ended in Afghanistan. (Bob O'Brien Collection)

In this photograph of 60204, traces of the original Thai Airways scheme can be seen. (Gerry Manning)

Philippine Airlines was a good customer for the 748, having operated a total of 21 aircraft. (David R Lawrence)

Series 2A 9N-AAV was delivered new to Royal Nepal Airlines in March 1970 and served with them for 30 years. It was finally broken up for spares in 2009. (Bob O'Brien Collection)

Chapter 4
Australasia and Oceania

Royal Australian Armed Forces

The RAAF was an early customer for the Series 2 748s. The first two aircraft were delivered in March and May 1967, with an 18-seat VIP fitting. A further eight aircraft were delivered between mid-1968 and mid-1969 to the School of Air Navigation in Victoria. Several of them were configured as flying classrooms for the training of RAAF and Royal Australian Navy (RAN) personnel. All the aircraft saw regular service throughout their lives, with the two VIP versions in particular flying to nations in the Pacific, New Guinea, and New Zealand. The last four aircraft were retired on 30 June 2004, after carrying out a unique formation flight over their native Victoria.

During their 37 years with the Air Force, the aircraft had not only carried out training and VIP duties. They were often called upon to deal with emergency situations, such as Cyclone Tracy, which hit Darwin in 1974, and for several months in 1989, during a dispute with Australian pilots, they were able to offer relief flights to cities in the south of Australia.

Two Series 2A aircraft were also ordered by the RAN. These were delivered during May and August 1973. As with so many 748s, they were used to replace DC-3s that had been used as electronic warfare trainers, being fitted with electronic countermeasures equipment and chaff (thin, narrow metallic strips capable of forming false echoes to radar equipment) dispensers, in order to present themselves as hostile aircraft. They remained in service until June 2000. Although the 748 found favour with the Australian Armed Forces, it is fair to say that generally, it did not sell to the major carriers. Part of the reason for this is the sheer distances involved in Australian air travel.

A10-605, a Series 2 of the RAAF 32 Sqn, on display at Avalon, Victoria, in 2003. (Gerry Manning)

Avro 748

Another view of this aircraft in immaculate condition. The RAAF loved its Avros. (Gerry Manning)

Nowra, New South Wales, is the home base of this Series 2 Royal Australian Navy electronic countermeasures aircraft. (Lloyd P Robinson)

N15-710 served with the Royal Australian Navy for 27 years before being broken up in 2001. (Lloyd P Robinson)

Formerly Royal Australian Navy N15-709, this Series 2 was awaiting an LFD conversion that never took place. (Lloyd Robinson)

Above: VH-IMI and VH-IMK parked together at Bankstown, New South Wales. They were leased from BAe to carry out newspaper flights. (Lloyd P Robinson)

Left: A 10-601 looks almost artificial beneath a protective cover at the RAAF museum in Point Cook, Victoria. (Lloyd P Robinson)

Below: A10-602 was one of several Series 2s delivered to the RAAF in 1968. (David R Lawrence)

Airline of the Marshall Islands

Located in the Pacific Ocean, near to the Equator and slightly to the west of the International Date Line, lie the Marshall Islands, a sleepy archipelago consisting of 29 coral atolls spread across several thousand miles of the mid-Pacific basin and particularly subject to fluctuating tides; the highest point is just 7ft above sea level. The country is part of the Micronesia island group.

Airline of the Marshall Islands (AMI) was established in 1980, as a company wholly owned by the government of the Marshall Islands. A requirement for an aircraft to serve the outer islands and atolls was identified and an invitation to tender was issued by the Marshall Islands government. It was against this background that it ordered a Series 2B in 1982. The operation had previously been carried out by the short-term operation of an Australian-built Government Aircraft Factories Nomad around the islands. However, the 748 was the first to join the fleet permanently, purchased specifically to link the larger islands in the chain, including Enewetak and Bikini Atoll (after which the bathing suit is named), which lay more than 500 miles (805km) north of the capital, Majuro.

All contracts for new aircraft are subject to a considerable amount of negotiation and a team was put together and based at Majuro for this purpose. One of the biggest difficulties that the team faced was communication. Majuro's only link with the outside world at the time was by high-frequency (HF) radio. Whilst still a useful medium even today, HF is subject to the vagaries of Equatorial weather and, of course, is totally insecure, so the team would have to fly the 1,000-mile (1,610km) round trip to Nauru once a week in order to communicate with the factory by phone and/or fax. Since Nauru is 12 hours ahead of the UK, this required a considerable adjustment to sleeping patterns.

The contract negotiations took six months, resulting in frequent visits to the islands. The Marshall Islands were reached from the UK via either Hong Kong or Honolulu, depending on other ongoing negotiations. The deal was finally concluded and an interim lease of the current demonstrator at the time, G-BGJV, was agreed until the ordered aircraft could be delivered. Most of the runways in the chain, apart from those at the main airports in Majuro and Kwajalein, were formed of compacted coral, and approach aids were non-existent. Only Majuro had a non-directional beacon (NDB) installed and this was at the other end of the atoll. At night-time, the runway lights would only be illuminated once contact with the NDB had been established, which led to a few missed approaches in the early days of operation.

MI 8203 was one of five registrations allocated to this aircraft during its lifetime. (Bob O'Brien Collection)

Subsequently registered MI 8203, the aircraft was re-registered V7-8203 in early 1993, when it went on a partial lease to Royal Tongan Airlines, carrying the Tongan colours on the port side and the revised AMI colours to starboard. The aircraft was finally sold to South Africa in 1999.

Mount Cook Airlines – New Zealand

Mount Cook, known locally as Aoraki, is situated in the centre of the South Island and is the highest mountain in New Zealand. It sits at a height of 12,218ft (3,724m) and forms part of what is known as the Southern Alps, which run throughout the length of the South Island. The area forms part of a national park and is popular with hikers and sightseers. From these origins, and given the nature of the terrain, it was obvious that, with the popularity of the area and the potential difficulties of siting an airfield, a solution would nevertheless have to be found. Mount Cook Airfield was opened in the early 1960s. It is located at the end of a fjord and, when originally opened, was simply a grass strip. Although the airline was based in Christchurch, it had quickly identified the need for flights to the area and had begun operations with DC-3s in 1961. With a challenging approach, a height above sea level of 2,153ft (656m) and an available landing distance of just 4,833ft (1,473m), the airfield was ideal for a 748 operation. Mount Cook Airlines ordered a Series 2-type aircraft, later converted to a Series 2A, which arrived in Christchurch on 5 October 1968. When it arrived in New Zealand, the 748 had been configured for 52 passengers. Soon afterwards, the seating was reduced to 46 and, ultimately, to 44 in mid-1969, to enable more storage space for skis. On most routes, the 748 was configured for 48 passengers. The introduction of the 748 on the Mount Cook route was extraordinarily successful and the passenger figures grew rapidly. Such was the reliability of the 748 that it was frequently used to cover the unserviceability of the Boeing 737-200s and F-27-100s owned by the New Zealand National Airways Corporation. A further two Series 2A aircraft were ordered and delivered in July 1971 and September 1973. A further aircraft was bought from Hawker Siddeley in September 1976. This happened to be the former Howard Hughes aircraft. Additionally, another Series 2A was leased from Polynesian Airlines from June to October in 1982, to cover the busy ski season. Other aircraft were leased to cope with additional seasonal traffic. But changes were ahead, and Mount Cook became a subsidiary of Air New Zealand on 1 April 1991. The last 748, ZK-MCA, left service in 1999, replaced by the ATR-72, carrying Air New Zealand Link colours. Gone was the familiar white petal logo from the tailplane of Mount Cook's aircraft, known as the Mount Cook lily.

Air New Zealand continued the service to Mount Cook Airfield until 2002, when the wooden terminal building, built to blend in with the local surroundings, was destroyed by arson. The operator has now decided to discontinue flights to the airfield, citing lack of demand.

ZK-MCA seen during a turnaround at Mount Cook Airfield. (Steve Lowe)

Right: Sitting next to 'big brother', ZK-MCF was one of eight 748s that Mount Cook operated. The airline was eventually taken over by Air New Zealand. (Steve Lowe)

Below: Mount Cook had not had time to repaint ZK-MCJ. It was placed into immediate service after its purchase from Air Pacific. (Steve Lowe)

Polynesian Airlines

The carrier was formed in 1959. It ordered two 748 Series 2As, which were delivered in January and November 1972. These were used on services based on the island of Apia (Samoa) to connect with nearby islands, such as Nandi, Pago Pago and Wallis Island. The name was changed to Samoa Airlines in 2017.

The Apia–Nandi (Fiji)–Apia flight was unique in that it crossed the International Date Line. In the days of the 748 operation, it would depart Apia at 1330hrs and arrive in Nandi at 1630hrs the following day, having undertaken a three-hour flight. Equally, the return journey would find passengers arriving a day earlier than they left. The 748 operated with Polynesian Airlines until June 1982, when it was replaced by a Boeing 737-200. The carrier is now a purely local carrier operating between Pago Pago and Apia and offering ad hoc charters with DHC-6 Twin Otters.

On 31 December 2011, Samoa changed its time zone from universal time coordinated (UTC) -11 to UTC +13. This had the effect of jumping forward a complete day and omitting 30 December from the calendar. Not only that, but it meant that the International Date Line had to be changed, moving the line to the east of the nation. The change was made to make doing business with Australasia easier as, previously, Samoa was 21 hours behind Sydney. The change means it is now three hours ahead.

Horizon Airlines – Australia

Headquartered in Sydney, this operator concentrated on cargo work, having bought two standard 748s, one a Series 2A and the other a Series 2B. On arrival in Australia, they were fitted with reinforced floors and LFDs in order for them to handle containerised cargo. The airline purchased two further Series 2Bs in 1999, with one being broken up for spares and the second aircraft having a standard 44-seat configuration and offered for ad hoc charters. In April 2003, Horizon was sold to MacAir Airlines based in Queensland, but by the end of that year, the 748s were no longer in operation. During this time, a total of ten aircraft had passed through the operator's hands. Most were broken up for spares.

Left: Series 2 VQ-FAL, carrying its pre-independence registration prefix, is readied for the long ferry flight to its new owners. (David R Lawrence)

Below: VH-IMK was originally G-BCOF, as part of the British Airways Highlands and Islands fleet. It is seen here at Bankstown Airport in Sydney, awaiting an LFD conversion. (Brian R Robinson)

Chapter 5
North America

Airline Deregulation Act

The Airline Deregulation Act of 1978 was critical in the attempts of all manufacturers to sell commuter type aircraft in the US. The act specified that the Civil Aeronautics Board (CAB), who had previously overseen route applications, would eventually be closed – known within the business as 'The CAB Sunset'. Previously, there had been strict controls on airline operators and routes, which meant that in order to serve a given route, regulatory approval had to be given by the CAB. Thus, an existing operator could, and almost certainly would, object to another carrier that applied to operate on its routes, thus stifling potential competition. The CAB was finally dismantled on 1 January 1985, which led to a seismic shift in the way airlines in the US operated.

The larger airlines quickly moved to what became known as hub-and-spoke operations, whereby a large airport, for example Atlanta, would be selected as the hub from which services would operate to other hubs in order for the traffic to be fed to smaller airports. This avoided the previous practice of operating a point-to-point route that did not have high load factors. Additionally, passengers arriving on flights from outside the US would find it significantly easier to reach the smaller towns and cities within the US, with no requirement for a second check-in, and baggage tagged through to the final destination.

The one flaw in this idea was that, by tradition, the carriers had typically operated larger aircraft, such as DC-8s, DC-9s, and Boeing 727 and 737s, on most of their routes. These were fine for the longer flights, but inefficient for much of the 'spoke' traffic. It was at this point that what became known as commuter aircraft came into their own. Some carriers had already bought aircraft and begun routes in anticipation of the act, and others quickly followed, ordering the Fokker F-27, the Shorts 360, the Embraer Bandeirante and another BAe product, the Jetstream, built at their Prestwick factory in Scotland. Locally sourced Beech 1900s were much in evidence, as well. Against this background, BAe began a series of demonstrations to the emerging second-level carriers in the US, but by the time the Deregulation Act had been fully enforced, it was becoming rapidly apparent that the hub-and-spoke system was a huge success, and that there was a demand for larger capacity, even on the smaller spoke routes, and thus, in many cases, the older jets returned to these services. As passenger figures began to increase, the larger airlines – the so-called 'legacy carriers' – bought out many of the feeder airlines, in order to have full control over ticketing, revenue and day-to-day operations. Thus, the bonanza that the builders of commuter aircraft had hoped for never fully materialised, but the whole process of deregulation was a bonus for travellers, with lower ticket prices and improved services.

Air Virginia

Based in Lynchburg, Virginia, Air Virginia began operating with a Piper Navajo from Lynchburg to Washington National Airport. The network expanded rapidly to include flights from Newark to North Carolina and as far west as Ohio. Air Virginia took delivery of two Series 2Bs, one in October 1981 and a second in May 1982. The Air Illinois Series 2B N749LL was also leased between August 1983 and June 1984. In May 1985, the airline became part of American Eagle. Both aircraft were returned to BAe in late 1984. One was leased to Azorean-based SATA and the other was used as a development aircraft before being sold.

Air Illinois

Air Illinois was probably unique in that, during most of its existence, it did not operate any aircraft that had been manufactured in the US. The carrier began operations in August 1970, based in Carbondale, Illinois, almost 300 miles (480km) south of Chicago. Initial routes linked nearby cities and then began expanding further south into Kentucky, Missouri, and Iowa in the northwest.

One of its prime routes was into Meigs Field, Chicago, and the 748 had been chosen for its ability to operate easily in and out of this airfield. The airfield had begun life in 1948 as a peninsula, having been built from reclaimed land on the shores of Lake Michigan, very close to Chicago itself. The runway had been extended by degrees, with a final length of 3,900ft (1,189m) being achieved. The airline had taken delivery of a Series 2A (N748LL) in October 1973, with the specific intention of using it for operation into this airfield. In December 1980, it took delivery of a second aircraft, a Series 2B, N749LL. The 748 was the largest aircraft to operate scheduled services into Meigs Field.

Tragedy befell Air Illinois on 11 October 1983, when N748LL crashed on approach into the home base at Carbondale. The aircraft was written off and a subsequent FAA investigation into the accident resulted in Air Illinois having its operating certificate revoked. The airline handed back its operating licence on 14 December 1983, with the second aircraft having already been returned to BAe in October 1982. The accident aside, the fact that Air Illinois had stopped operating large aircraft into Meigs gave Mayor Daley a long-sought opportunity to close the airfield. The airfield was finally turned into a public park two years later. We can only speculate whether the destruction of Meigs would have taken place if Air Illinois had continued to operate its scheduled services into what was clearly a very convenient downtown airport.

Cascade Airways

Cascade was formed in in 1969 in Spokane, Washington, on the west coast of the US. The backbone of the fleet was the Beech 99, with a total of 15 aircraft having operated for the airline. They operated primarily in the northwest of the US, connecting towns and cities in the nearby states of Idaho, Oregon, and Montana, and with an international route to Calgary, Canada. It took delivery of two 748 Series 2Bs in December 1981. An option was placed on a third aircraft, but this was never taken up. Its biggest competitor was Horizon Air, which began operating in 1981. Horizon was well-financed and able to purchase both Air Oregon in 1982 and Transwestern Airlines in 1983. The effect was crippling for Cascade, and, in 1985, it approached Horizon with a view to an eventual buy-out, but a deal could not be reached, and Cascade was forced to file for Chapter 11 bankruptcy in March 1986. The aircraft were sold to Bradley Air Services in Canada.

Cascade Airways operated two 748 Series 2As. Here, N117CA is seen taxiing in at Seattle-Tacoma Airport in 1984. (Gerry Manning)

Canada

Canada was a huge market for used 748s. With its dozens of remote settlements, most of them with unpaved airfields, the 748 was an ideal choice. Particularly sought-after were those with LFDs. Such was the demand for LFDs that when word reached Air Inuit that a LIAT Series 2A, V2-LAZ, the only one in the fleet that had been fitted with an LFD, was being ferried to Woodford after being taken in part-exchange for new 748 2Bs, was for sale, the ferry flight was diverted to Montreal, where the aircraft was sold on the spot. The pilots, somewhat to their surprise, instead of routing home via Newfoundland, Greenland, and Iceland, found themselves booked on a scheduled British Airways flight to Manchester. Given the difficult operating conditions in northern Canada, it made sense for them to buy aircraft from previous operators, rather than new ones.

This was a situation in which the carriage of passengers was less important than that of cargo; food, building materials and, often, fuel would regularly be carried, since this was the quickest and easiest way to convey it. Some of the major operations take place in the Northwest Territories. For an idea of the distances involved within this area of Canada, it can perhaps be understood when considering that this province alone is the size of France, Portugal and Spain combined. Next-door lies Nunavut. Although the second least populous of Canada's provinces, with a population of just 36,000, in terms of land area, Nunavut is only slightly smaller than Mexico. If it were a country, it would rank 15th in area in the world. It is the mineral wealth in the area that draws people there. The industry, whilst in itself is a customer for the airlines that service it with equipment, also requires settlements. People have to eat, build, heat houses and live as normal a daily life as possible, despite the hostile conditions. It is no exaggeration to say that airlines such as Calm Air, Air Creebec, First Air and Kelner (now Wasaya) provide a lifeline to Inuit communities throughout Canada. One of the regular cargoes is fuel, and several aircraft have been adapted to carry large tanks capable of carrying up to 7,500 litres of diesel and fuel oil.

Nowadays, the 748 is generally used as a pure cargo aircraft, hence the interest in the LFD versions. There are now only two operators with aircraft based in the region. These are Air Inuit, based in Kuujjuaq, Quebec, and Wasaya, in Thunder Bay. Most now fly unpressurised. Not using the pressurisation enables the life of the aircraft to be prolonged. No less than 62 748s have appeared on the Canadian register, a testament to the versatility and popularity of the aircraft.

C-GMAA, a Series 2, is seen here at Pickle Lake, Ontario, in its modified version for use by Air Creebec. The aircraft is a pure freighter, with no windows and no pressurisation. (Gerry Manning)

Avro 748

Another view of C-GMAA, which still carries the same registration, but is now operated by Wasaya Airways. (Gerry Manning)

Air Manitoba operated seven Series 2A 748s. C-FAGI is seen here at Winnipeg. The airline ceased operating in 1995. (Gerry Manning)

Although not fitted with a freight door, this Series 2 is only used for carrying freight. It is seen here at Pickle Lake, Ontario. (Gerry Manning)

Another view of C-GLTC. The aircraft was formerly owned by the Bundesanstalt für Flugsicherung (German Air Traffic Control) in Germany. (Gerry Manning)

Avro 748

The same aircraft, C-GLTC, now carrying the colours of Inter City Airways. The nature of operations in Canada is such that the aircraft are often moved between carriers. (Gerry Manning)

A very smart Air North Series 2, C-FAGI, rests between flights at Fairbanks, Alaska, in May 2000. (Gerry Manning)

Another view of C-FAGI at Fairbanks, Alaska, in 2000. (Gerry Manning)

Another Canadian operator, First Air, operated C-GDUN, seen here between flights at Yellowknife, Northwest Territories, in 2000. (Gerry Manning)

Avro 748

Another of the First Air fleet, C-GGNZ, awaits its next flight at Yellowknife, Northern Territories. (Gerry Manning)

Stablemate C-GBFA is also hangared, no doubt with the harsh Canadian winter in mind. (Gerry Manning)

Three 748s for the price of one: looking across the apron at Sept-Îles Airport, Canada, from underneath another 748. (Author)

CF-TAZ was one of the few 748s to go on the Canadian register as a new aircraft. It was leased to Transair for a short time before being moved on to Philippine Airlines. (David R Lawrence)

Avro 748

Following service with Channel Airways, G-ATEJ was sold to Midwest and later re-registered as CF-MAL. (David R Lawrence)

Obviously, Transair did not believe in putting large registrations on its aircraft. This Series 2 example was bought in December 1967. (Bob O'Brien Collection)

Calm Air

If your name is Carl Arnold Lawrence Morberg and you decide to start an airline, then you are absolutely entitled to call it Calm Air, and that is just what he did. In 1962, he set up an airline with that name, ultimately turning it one of Canada's largest privately owned regional airlines. Based in Winnipeg, it serves the main towns of Manitoba, in addition to Canada's more remote areas, including Inuit settlements in Nunavut (originally part of the Northwest Territories). A total of 11 748s passed through the airline's hands, including several that operated in a combi configuration. Many of the airfields on the network, even today, have gravel strips, so the 748 was ideal for their operations. The aircraft operated between the late 1980s and early 1990s. Principal passenger flights are now conducted by ATR 42 and 72s. The company was taken over in April 2009 by a holding company that also controls Perimeter Airlines and Keewatin Air, both of which are based in Winnipeg.

Right: C-FMAK was one of 11 748s that passed through Calm Air's hands. The airline operated scheduled services throughout Manitoba and Hudson Bay. (Bob O'Brien Collection)

Below: Calm Air's 748s looked very smart in the Canadian Airlines livery. This Series 2A was originally delivered to Ghana Airways. (Bob O'Brien Collection)

Air Gaspé

The headquarters of this little-known airline were in Sept-Îles, Quebec. The airline provided charter flights, beginning in 1951, and in 1973, became a subsidiary of Quebecair, although it continued to use the Air Gaspé titles. The airline operated both scheduled passenger and cargo flights from Gaspé, a tourist town in the far northeast of the Quebec province and acquired a single 748 Series 2A, registered CF-AGI, which was delivered in April 1971. The aircraft operated as far south as the Bahamas, but much of its work was concentrated in Quebec. From time to time, the aircraft would be chartered by deer hunters and some of the seats would be taken out in order to accommodate the carcasses they had bagged. The conditions under which the aircraft was operated were particularly harsh; because of its location, the area suffers extremes of climate. For example, there was no hangar at the base and all scheduled and unscheduled maintenance had to be carried out in the open. The aircraft was eventually absorbed into the Quebecair fleet in early 1984 and, by this time, had been re-registered as C-FAGI. It was later owned by Air Manitoba and Wasaya Airways before being sold to Air North in 1998.

Canadian Pacific Airlines

It might be surprising to learn that the 748 played its part in the huge transport undertaking that Canadian Pacific became. The airline was renamed CP Air in 1968 and the aircraft acquired a new orange livery. This lasted until January 1986, when the airline reverted to its original name, Canadian Pacific Airlines (CPA), following the takeover of Eastern Provincial Airways (EPA), which had begun life as a regional carrier based in Gander. It is at this point that the 748 becomes involved in the story. EPA had always bought 748s from the pre-owned market, and the first one to appear, C-FINE, a Series 2 that had been modified to Series 2A, came from Inexco Oil, an oil and gas exploration company based in Houston, Texas, and was delivered in 1975. Six further used aircraft followed from various sources. All had been modified to Series 2A before delivery. EPA also leased aircraft, including

Sister ship N118CA, also at Seattle-Tacoma, which was a major destination for Cascade. (Gerry Manning)

three from the manufacturer, and it leased several aircraft out to operators abroad. The routes flown were mainly within eastern Canada. The CPA name was short-lived, however. In 1987, CPA was sold to Pacific Western Airlines based in the western city of Calgary, and as the takeover took hold, the 748s began to be sold off, with the last aircraft leaving service in late 1986. Shortly afterwards, the name was changed, yet again, to Canadian Airlines, which, in turn, was merged into Air Canada in 2000.

Between April 1987 and early 1990, several Calm Air aircraft also carried the Canadian Airlines scheme, as a result of a 45 per cent share purchase by the larger carrier in Calm Air. After the takeover of Canadian Airlines by Air Canada, the schedules ran with the 'AC' prefix, but in April 2002, the Morberg family bought back the 45 per cent shareholding and the flight reverted to the 'MO' prefix.

Right: First Air Series 2A C-GFNW sits in the hangar at Yellowknife. Like many of the 748s that operated in Canada, this one was equipped with an LFD. (Gerry Manning)

Below: C-GDUN taxies out from Hay River in Canada's Northwest Territories, helping to keep remote communities connected. (Gerry Manning)

The propeller tips create a visible vortex as the final North Air flight leaves the airfield. (Air North/Simon Blakesley)

A final salute from the last Air North 748, C-FCSE, as it does a low pass at Yellowknife. (Air North/Simon Blakesley)

Chapter 6

Latin America and the Caribbean

The vastness of the larger South American nations meant that moving about was always going to be a difficult and time-consuming business. As in other countries, fledgling operators had bought surplus equipment from World War Two and begun to operate it on the longer distances, especially to those areas that were not accessible by railways. Airfields were rudimentary, the runway often consisting of a dirt strip and a control tower atop a small, square building that doubled as a passenger terminal. Airfield equipment would be poor or non-existent and navigation equipment carried on the aircraft that served them would be rudimentary at best.

As in other countries, the DC-3 had become the aircraft of choice, but, being unpressurised, they would have to fly through, or very close to, the storms that frequently occurred. Equally, although the DC-3s and other types were reliable, they had a finite life, and the larger airlines began to look at replacements.

One of two Series 2As operated by COPA Panama, HP-484 is seen at Tocumen Airport. The aircraft later became G-BCDZ. (4 Aviation)

Final approach in a Guyana Airways 748 to the airstrip at Lethem, Guyana. The airfield now has a paved runway. (Author)

Avro 748

The locals turn out to greet the scheduled 748 flight at Lethem on Guyana's Brazilian border. (Author)

C6-BEF at Marsh Harbour on the Abaco Islands in the Bahamas. The striking colour scheme was designed by the PR team at Woodford. (Author)

The terminal building at Lethem. The large bulldozer to the left of the building was used for grading the runway. (Author)

First painted as C6-BEA, a standard Series 2A, it sits at Miami in the original Bahamasair colour scheme. The aircraft served for 14 years before being sold in Canada. (Bob O'Brien Collection)

Avro 748

V2-LIK was one of the aircraft replaced by the Series 2Bs in 1985. Prior to sale, it had accumulated the highest number of landings of any 748, at just under 75,000. The registration is now worn by an ATR 42. (Bob O'Brien Collection)

The short runway at Beef Island, the largest of the British Virgin Islands, meant that the types of aircraft that could use it were limited, but the 748 was one that could. (Bob O'Brien Collection)

LAN-Chile was an early customer for the 748. This Series 2 is seen at Los Cerrillos, the former downtown airport in Santiago, Chile. (Bob O'Brien Collection)

Clearly out of its comfort zone, Cayman Airways Series 1 VR-CBH sits outside the Dan-Air maintenance hangar at Manchester. (Keir Faulkner)

LAN-Chile took delivery of this Series 2 example in November 1968. They were largely used on domestic services. (David R Lawrence)

The original Avianca colour scheme was applied to this Series 2A before delivery in 1968. (David R Lawrence)

Right: The cheat line had not yet been applied to this Avianca Series 2A, one of two ordered new by the airline. (David R Lawrence)

Below: VP-BCJ carries its pre-independence registration and the 'Speedbird' logo on the tail, emphasising the close connection with BOAC. The Bahamas was later allocated 'C6-' as its ICAO prefix. (David R Lawrence)

The later Avianca scheme has been applied to this Series 2A, HK 1409, originally delivered in October 1968. (Bob O'Brien Collection)

Aerolíneas Argentinas

The first airline to look closely at the 748 was Aerolíneas Argentinas (AA), who, having seen the aircraft demonstrated on its own territory, decided that it was right for them. For reference, Argentina's land mass is four times that of France, so there is a lot of land to cover. The airline ordered a batch of nine Series 1 aircraft, which were delivered during 1962. The world's first revenue service by a 748 was operated on 2 April 1962, when LV-HGW flew from Buenos Aires' downtown airport at Aeroparque Jorge Newbery. With nine aircraft, AA was able to rapidly expand the route network both within Argentina and to neighbouring countries, such as Paraguay and Uruguay.

The success of the operation led to AA ordering a further three aircraft and these were delivered in the latter part of 1963. Almost every country in South America has suffered from raging inflation in the past 50 years and Argentina is no exception. Its own currencies are often unconvertible or semi-convertible and, thus, the goods it buys can be significantly more expensive than the ticket price. Commercial aircraft around the world are invariably sold in dollars.

To help overcome this, AA came up with a novel idea. Knowing of the British love of corned beef and the Argentinians' ability to produce vast quantities of it, AA, since it was a government-owned airline, offered the product in part payment, known as countertrade. There is no record of exactly how many tins of corned beef were eventually traded, but one can imagine that there must have been many a ship's hold crammed with them in the early 1960s.

This aircraft was later registered LV-HGW and carried out the first commercial service with a 748 on 2 April 1962. (David R Lawrence)

Argentine Air Force (Fuerza Aérea Argentina)

In the years since the Falklands War, it is perhaps difficult to imagine how cordial the relations once were between Britain and Argentina. The British had built the railways and been involved in many other infrastructure projects throughout the country, including the docks in Buenos Aires. There was even the *Buenos Aires Herald*, a daily newspaper printed in English. With the Aerolíneas Argentinas deal under its belt, the 748 sales team targeted the Argentinian Air Force with a view to replacing its DC-3s. The Air Force had taken delivery of a VIP (serial T-01) version of the Series 2 for presidential use in 1966, so the negotiations for a further eight aircraft, in theory, were unlikely to be particularly difficult. In 1967, an order was placed for the transport division, but it was not to be. International politics intervened. The purchase order had been sent to the president for signing when foot-and-mouth disease broke out in Britain. The outbreak was blamed on contaminated Argentine meat, which naturally did not sit well with its government, and all potential deals for British goods were cancelled, with Fokker picking up the order. Initially, eight aircraft were ordered, followed by a further four, so the loss of business was significant.

Brazilian Air Force (FAB)

The second big order for the 748 came from the Brazilian Air Force. This was for six aircraft initially. These were Series 2 versions, with improved Dart engines, delivered between late 1962 and 1963. With the Brazilian capital having been transferred from Rio de Janeiro to Brasilia in 1960, there was a considerable requirement for travel between the two cities. They were used principally as communications aircraft, based at Galeão, Rio de Janeiro's international airport and operating throughout Brazil, though principally between Rio de Janeiro and Brasilia. The FAB was so happy with the aircraft that it followed this up with an order for a further six, which were delivered during 1975. These were different, in that all were fitted with an LFD.

Varig – Brazil

The other large order from Brazil came from the national airline Varig. In a similar way to Aerolíneas Argentinas, it had routes to the less-inhabited areas with rudimentary airfield facilities. Varig had operated a fleet of 21 DC-3s on the shorter routes throughout Brazil. It leased the second production aircraft, G-ARAY, between 1965 and 1966 and was sufficiently impressed to place an order for ten Series 2As. These were delivered between November 1967 and September 1968 and put into service

PP-VDO, the second aircraft for Varig, sits outside at Woodford prior to delivery in January 1968. (David R Lawrence)

Another Varig example, being prepared for engine runs prior to delivery. This aircraft was demonstrated to Avianca during its delivery flight. (David R Lawrence)

on Varig's extensive network throughout Brazil, often flying up to ten sectors per day. They were also used on the air-bridge route between Rio de Janeiro and São Paulo. The aircraft were popular with passengers and crews and became known as the 'Avro'. The demand for larger and faster aircraft meant that Varig began to dispose of them in 1975 and the last aircraft left service in 1977.

LAV – Venezuela/Fuerza Aérea Venezolana

For reasons best known to themselves, some of the LAV aircraft were interchanged with the military. Linea Aeropostal Venezolana, known simply as Aeropostal, was another major 748 operator. In terms of area, Venezuela is almost twice the size of Spain. Whilst there is an adequate road system, the few railway lines that existed were never developed, thus the quickest and easiest way around the country was by plane. Initially, Hawker Siddeley leased a 748 Series 2A (G-ARAY) between February and July 1965. An order for six Series 2As quickly followed and these were used mainly on domestic services, but with additional flights to Port of Spain in Trinidad, Georgetown in Guyana, and Curaçao in the Netherlands Antilles. A further two Series 2A aircraft were delivered in November 1976. In August 1966, a Series 2 aircraft had been ordered by the Venezuelan Ministry of Defence and given the serial 0111. Nominally, it was used by the president and used as a VIP transport. In stark contrast with other South American nations, Venezuela's continuous supply of petrodollars ensured that there were always funds for overseas purchases.

There are two airports in Caracas, Venezuela's capital. One is the major international airport on the coast, in the neighbourhood of Maiquetía, now renamed Simón Bolívar International Airport, and the other is the downtown airport in the suburb of La Carlota, now called Generalissimo Francisco de Miranda Air Base, after a Venezuelan revolutionary. This airport was used largely by the military, although private flying was allowed, and this is where 0111 was based. The airfield is situated at an elevation of 2,739ft (835m) above sea level and has a single runway of 6475ft (1974m) in length. Its operation is restricted by the surrounding mountains and is effectively daylight-only. Recent political disturbances in Venezuela have meant that the airfield is now used strictly for military and medical evacuation purposes.

The aircraft remained in service for 20 years before being transferred to LAV as YV-39C. However, it was damaged beyond repair in a ground accident and was later used as an instructional airframe. Another LAV aircraft went in the other direction. Having been delivered in July 1965 as YV-C-AMO, the aircraft suffered an accident some years later and, following repairs, was re-registered under the new system as YV-06C in 1975. In 1977, it was transferred to the Servicio de Aviación Naval Venezolana and carried the serial TR-0203 before being sold to Austin Airways in Canada in 1981.

A further aircraft that crossed the civil/military boundary was Series 2 YV-C-AMI (a registration used twice before on Lockheed Constellations), which was delivered to Aeropostal in 1965 and was involved in a bizarre taxiing accident when it was struck by a C-46 in April 1973. The aircraft was repaired and re-registered as YV-05C in 1975, before being leased to the Fuerza Aérea Venezolana for three years and given the serial 6201. It was returned to Aeropostal in May 1980 and was reallocated its previous registration but followed YV-06C just six months later to Austin Airways.

Trinidad and Tobago Air Services (TTAS)

Most airlines have a route network, but there is always an exception, and this was the case with TTAS. The airline was set up by the government of Trinidad and Tobago in 1974 to link the two islands. Originally, the service had been operated by a US-registered DC-6, but between December 1977 and November 1979, TTAS took delivery of six Series 2As, two of them fitted with LFDs. Any ferry service between the two islands was unreliable at best, so the provision of a 30-minute flight on what was now being called an 'air bridge' was very welcome. At its peak, the service operated eight flights a day in each direction. In 1980, TTAS was merged with British West Indian Airways (BWIA) in order to provide a more efficient service, and from 1984 onwards, the aircraft were used on wider services in the Caribbean, providing connecting flights to BWIA's services. During the mid-1980s, the runway and other facilities at Crown Point, Tobago's airport, were upgraded in order to handle jets. As a result, BWIA revised its schedules so that flights from Miami, for example, could route direct to Crown Point. This allowed BWIA to release the 748s on short-term leases. Disposal of the fleet began in the spring of 1986, with the last flight by a 748 in June 1986.

The Trinidad and Tobago registration applied to this Series 2A reveals that this aircraft was originally allocated to BWIA, but not taken up. It was re-registered as VP-LAA. (David R Lawrence)

Fuerza Aérea Ecuatoriana (FAE) – Ecuador

One of the major considerations during the design of the 748 was to ensure that it would be able to operate in airfields that are in hot and high areas. The combination of thin air and high temperatures causes a considerable loss of power to aircraft engines, often requiring the aircraft to carry a lesser payload, with a consequent loss of revenue. In Ecuador, many of the airfields fall into this category. The former international airport in the capital Quito was situated 9,228ft (2,813m) above sea level, and several of the country's airports lie at elevations above 4,000ft (1,220m).

The Air Force initially ordered four Series 2A aircraft, one of which became the presidential aircraft and as such carried two registrations, FAE 001 and HC-AUK, both of which were applied to the aircraft simultaneously. Two of these were fitted with an LFD, with the first two being delivered in 1970 and the second two in 1975 and 1976. The aircraft were later transferred to TAME (Transportes Aéreos Militares Equatorianas), which operated flights carrying civilians to the more remote areas of Ecuador, on routes that were not financially viable for a commercial operation. Several of the aircraft served with the operator for almost 44 years, with the last one only being withdrawn from service in August 2014.

Above: Originally delivered in 1970, the presidential 748 Series 2A carried two registrations because it was also used by TAME. (Gerry Manning)

Left: Another aircraft used by TAME, seen here at Mariscal Sucre International Airport, Quito. (Gerry Manning)

A TAME Series 2A carries both military and civil identification. Like SATENA, these aircraft fulfilled both civil and military functions. (Gerry Manning)

The unusual appearance of FAE 738, a Series 2A, was brought about by it being dropped accidentally whilst being carried by a helicopter. It was subsequently used as a parachute training aircraft. (Gerry Manning)

Above: FAE 738 sits in a quiet corner of the military area, having been turned into a parachute training aircraft after its accident. (Gerry Manning)

Left: Series 2A FAE 739 sits in a remote corner of the airport at Quito, minus its propellers. (Gerry Manning)

Carrying two identities, HC-AUK/FAE 684 now sits in the museum at Quito International Airport. (Gerry Manning)

SATENA – Colombia

SATENA operated in a similar way to TAME, in that its route network comprised the smaller and less accessible towns in Colombia. The country is divided by three mountain ranges and, like Ecuador, many of the airfields are 'hot and high'. SATENA ordered four 748 2As, all of which were delivered during March 1972 and registered FAC1101-4. Operations into the more remote airfields were often perilous, with a total absence of navigation or direction equipment to help the pilots. Many of the airfields were unpaved, and even those that were would only have a bare coating of tarmac, meaning that aquaplaning was always a possibility. Within two years, the first aircraft, FAC 1103, had crashed after failing to cross a high mountain in the Andes and a second aircraft, FAC 1104, was damaged beyond repair after it skidded off the runway at Pasto, an airfield located on a high plateau in the southeast of the country. The airfield is located at 5,951ft (1,814m) elevation and often subjected to bad weather. FAC 1102 was sold to West Air Sweden but was broken up for parts.

By far, the most bizarre accident took place with the first aircraft to be delivered, FAC-1101. A company mechanic, who had been dismissed some days earlier, entered the SATENA hangar early in the morning of 22 August 1979, took the aircraft out of the hangar and started it up. He was alone on the flight deck and did not contact air traffic control. By the time they realised what was happening, it was too late to stop him, and the aircraft became airborne and headed towards one of the principal avenues in the city. Possessing few flying skills and with minimum fuel in the tanks, he was unable to manoeuvre the aircraft and quickly lost control. He crashed onto a Bogotá suburb, killing himself and several people on the ground. It is believed that his intention was to crash the aircraft onto the house of either his parents or his girlfriend. With just one aircraft left of the original four, SATENA ordered another 748, this time a Series 2B equipped with an LFD. This aircraft was delivered in August 1981 and was given the serial number FAC-1108. SATENA was not the only operator of the 748 in Colombia. The national airline Avianca also purchased two new 748 Series 2As and had a third on lease for a while.

Parked in a remote corner of Bogotá Airport, FAC 1102 is seen here in 1992. Of the four Series 2As delivered to SATENA, this was the only one not to be written off. It was later sold to West Air Sweden. (Gerry Manning)

Above: FAC 1108 was one of the early Series 2Bs, seen here in 1992 at Villavicencio, still the haunt of DC-3s at the time. (Gerry Manning)

Left: FAC 1108 was the only Series 2B to be operated by SATENA. (Gerry Manning)

Below: The LFD is clearly visible on FAC 1108, the only SATENA 748 to have been fitted with one. (Gerry Manning)

FAC 1104, of SATENA, in its basic scheme at Medellín Airport. It was written off in an accident at Antonio Nariño Airport, Pasto, in 1983. (Werner Fischdick)

Above: FAC 1101 of SATENA was the aircraft that was stolen from the hangar by a disgruntled engineer and crashed onto houses in Bogotá, Colombia. (David R Lawrence)

Right: The original titling used the Colombian Air Force titles but was later changed in favour of SATENA. (David R Lawrence)

Demonstration Flights

With the 748 being perfectly adapted for operations in mountainous terrain, there was never any shortage of interest amongst potential and existing operators in the region, of which there were many, so the 748 demonstrator was a frequent visitor to Colombia. One of the more unusual demonstrations was to a company called Carbocol. A large deposit of high-grade coal had been discovered in an area of northeast Colombia, known as Cerrejón, near the Venezuelan border. The area lay in the largely uninhabited Guajira Peninsula in northeast Colombia, and the remoteness of the location meant there would clearly be difficulties in extracting the coal, in terms of moving both equipment and personnel. One solution that was being seriously considered was flying the personnel in and out to an airfield to be constructed near the site. The coal was on an open-cast site, so all the mining activity took place above ground. BAe (as it was by then) was approached by the company who were contracted to mine the coal, with a view to seeing whether it would be possible to operate a service whereby carrying the miners from a nearby large town would work. Accordingly, a demonstration was arranged. The gravel strip situated in the far northeast of Colombia was rudimentary to say the least. There were no approach aids, no buildings, simply a compacted strip made of fine gravel. The demonstration was successful, but the contractor chose the de Havilland Canada DHC-7 over the 748, on the not unreasonable grounds that, given the remote nature of the operation, four engines were safer than two.

The town of Mitú, Colombia, lies in the southeast of the country on the Amazon basin, a short distance from the Brazilian border. The town can only be reached by air or river because, even today, there are no roads out of the town. The airfield itself, in the 1980s, was rudimentary, with a strip that had been graded from soil and a simple building housing the control tower and offices. Unusually, the runway dissects the township and is situated close to the river. At the time, there was no scheduled air service. Almost all flights were cargo, carrying local produce from the plains to the major cities.

Most of these were operated by C-46s, often preferred over the DC-3 by cargo operators in the more mountainous areas of South America because of its more powerful engines and greater lifting capability. A demonstration had been requested by an operator called Servicios del Aéreos Vaupes (SELVA) based in Mitú. Coincidentally, in Spanish, the word *selva* means 'jungle'. Since there was already a demonstration booked for the Cerrejón project, this was included in the tour. The owners had seen the SATENA operation and believed that the 748 would offer a useful replacement. The company operated several C-46s, but these were now nearing the end of their lives and a replacement was being sought. A demonstration, again on an unpaved runway, took place, but the airline was unable to raise sufficient funds to buy the aircraft. It now operates several Antonov 26s.

G-BKAL attracts a crowd of locals during a demonstration in Mitú, Colombia, in 1983. (Author)

Above: The 748 demonstrates its rough-field capability during a take-off from the dusty unpaved strip at Mitú. (Author)

Right: The prospective customers arrived in Mitú in this C-46A HK-851. (Author)

Below: Another Colombian airfield, another demonstration. This was in the north of Colombia in the province of Cerrejón. (Author)

The demonstrator taxies out to take off from the gravel strip at Cerrejón. (Author)

Airborne, G-BKAL begins the demo. Sadly, this aircraft, as G-OJEM, was written off in an accident at Stansted in 1998, whilst carrying the Leeds United Football Club team. (Author)

A typical take-off run at Cerrejón. The strip was simply graded, and fine gravel was laid on top. (Author)

The two DHC Dash 7s, which won the Cerrejón contract, parked at Panama en route to their final destination. (Author)

Another country that received a number of demonstrations was Bolivia, principally to the national carrier, Lloyd Aéreo Boliviano (LAB). The highest international airport in the world is in the capital, La Paz. Appropriately called *El Alto* (The High One), it sits on a plateau higher than the city itself at 13,325ft (4,061m) elevation and is perhaps one of the few airports in the world with a fully functioning medical centre, ready to deal with the altitude sickness to which many visitors succumb. In a country where several of the other cities' main airports are situated above 6,000ft (1,830m), logically the 748 would be a perfect fit. Because of this, all LAB maintenance had to be carried out at Santa Cruz, which is a mere 1,225ft (373m) above sea level. LAB operated both the Fairchild (F-27J) and Fokker versions of the F-27. All but two of the six F-27Js were sourced from the used market, and, of the three F-27s, one was donated by Fokker, with one sourced from the used market and the other transferred from the military transport wing of the Bolivian Air Force, Transporte Aéreo Militar. All were used on domestic services, usually at the country's lower airports, and given the altitude of the larger cities, LAB preferred to use jets – normally the Boeing 727-100s – on the major domestic routes, with CP-1227 recording the highest number of cycles (the number of take-offs and landings) of any 727 before it was retired in 2005.

From this, it can be seen that LAB was rarely in the market for new aircraft. Bolivia was one of the poorest countries in South America and the problem of currency conversion dogged them even more seriously than it did other countries in the region. The fact that one of the freight operators was still operating B-17s in the mid-1980s perhaps gives some indication of the level of operation amongst the smaller operators, most of who preferred the C-46, with its useful lifting capacity of seven tonnes and plentiful inexpensive spares. LAB was wound up in 2010. It was the second oldest (Avianca is the oldest) airline in Latin America, having been founded in 1925.